PINNER

Hatch End, North Harrow and Rayners Lane

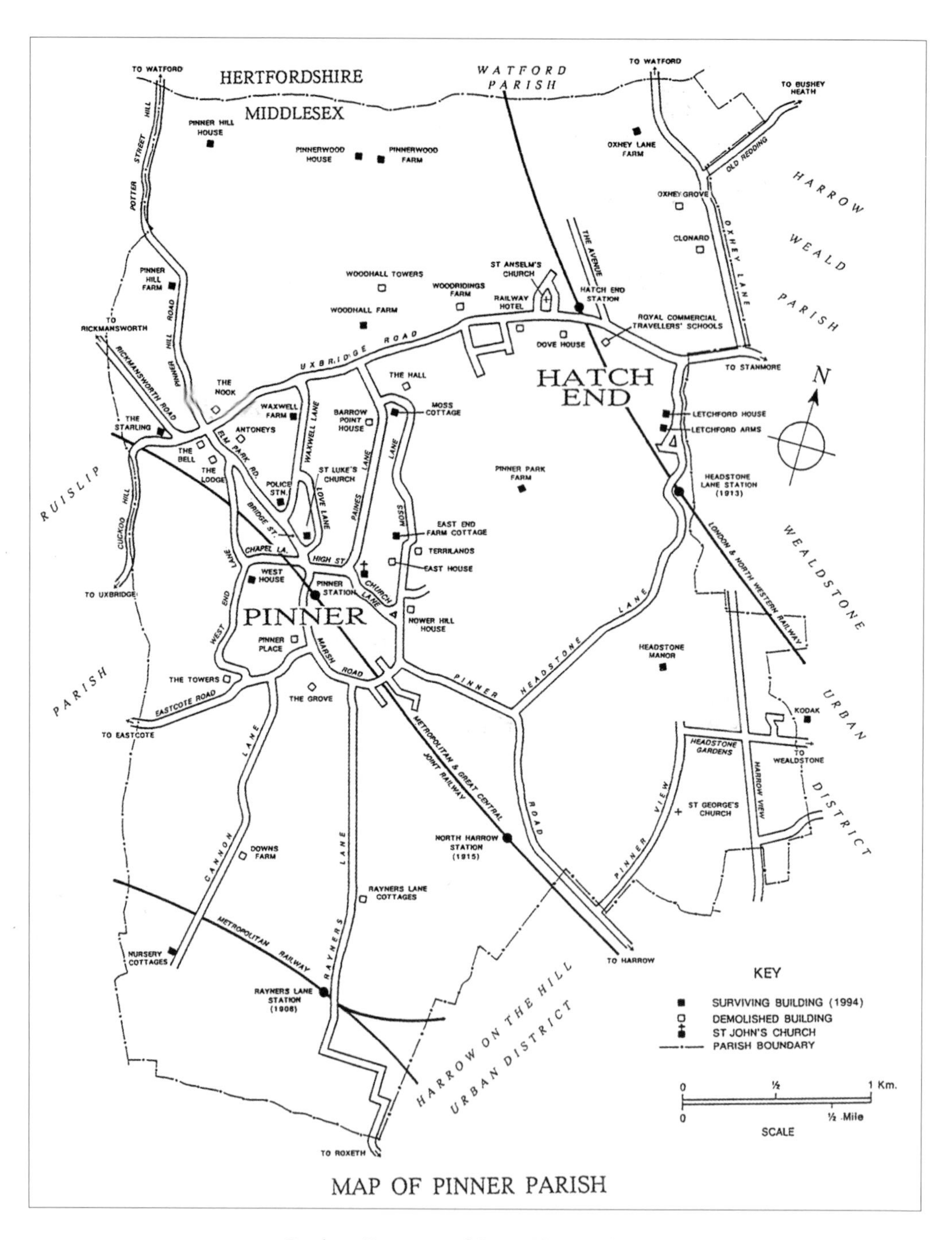

Guide to Location of Some Places in Text

PINNER
Hatch End, North Harrow and Rayners Lane

Patricia A. Clarke

Phillimore

2007

Published by
PHILLIMORE & CO. LTD
Chichester, West Sussex, PO20 2DD
www.phillimore.co.uk

ISBN 978-1-86077-465-2

Printed and bound in Great Britain

List of Illustrations

Acknowledgements

When Pinner Local History Society produced *A Pictorial History of Pinner, Hatch End, North Harrow and Rayners Lane* in 1994, a second book was not contemplated. Since then enough new pictures have become available to make a second one worthwhile. No picture from the first book is repeated in the second, which explains the absence of some that might be considered logical, such as the earliest photographs of St John's Church. The introduction to the first book covered the whole of Pinner's history, while this one concentrates on the last 200 years. These two books do not therefore fit neatly together but should be regarded as complementary to each other.

New pictures are included in family collections given or copied to us. In recent years we have been given papers of the late and indefatigable Jim Golland. The late David Bednall was an avid photographer in the 1970s and 1980s, and his pictures are now with us. Cyril Ellement, almost the last member of his family to live in Pinner, gave us his papers before he died. Members Frank Palmer, Sylvia Venis and Hilary Thornley have generously allowed us full access to their postcard collections. The Pinner Association has let us reproduce pictures from *The Villager*, and from its two *Panoramas of Pinner Village*, published in 1947 and 1969 respectively. It would be difficult to produce an illustrated book without some recourse to Harrow Libraries Local History Collection and to its keeper Bob Thomson, always helpful and accommodating. That collection includes the papers of Edwin Ware, whose lifetime hobby was the history of his beloved Pinner and who took many photographs himself. I have had enormous help from Graham Elcombe and Ken Kirkman as readers, and without them this book would have more mistakes and errors than I hope is the case. The map of Pinner was drawn by the late Tony Venis.

Illustration Acknowledgements

The illustrations are reproduced by kind permission of the following, to whom any application for use should be made: Mr and Mrs D. Brown, 168; Mrs Patricia Clarke, 2, 4, 30, 42, 45, 48, 50, 53, 69, 71, 94, 97, 101, 106, 126, 130, 146, 157; English Heritage, NMR, 27; Mrs A. Gibson, 183; Guildhall Library, City of London, 128; Michael Hammerson, 89, 170, 198; *Harrow Observer*, 216-17; Ken Kirkman, 5, 111-13, 115; London Borough of Harrow Local History Collection, 12, 16, 20-1, 29, 37, 63-4, 68, 70, 90-2, 107, 119, 122, 129, 136, 138, 142, 165-7, 186-8, 190-1, 200; Mrs Fiona Mallinson, 76-9, 108; Arthur W.J.G. Ord-Hume, 114, 116, 124, 154, 214; Frank Palmer, 1, 33, 62, 152, 201; Mrs Jette Parsey, 131; Pinner Association, 3, 31, 35, 47, 52, 82, 123, 189, 212; Pinner Local History Society, 6-11, 14, 17-19, 22-4, 26, 28, 32, 34, 43-4, 46, 49, 51, 55-61, 66-7, 72, 74-5, 81, 83-4, 87, 93, 95-6, 109-10, 120, 125, 127, 133-5, 137, 143, 145, 148-50, 153, 156, 158-9, 160-4, 169, 171-6, 178, 180-2, 184-5, 192-4, 196-7, 199, 202-11, 213, 215, 218; Mrs Helen Pugh, 98-100; F.R. Ree, 103-5; Mrs Claire Shaw, 39-41; The Grail, 151; Hilary Thornley, 13, 15, 25, 38, 54, 73, 85, 88, 118, 177, 179, 195; Michael Treisman, 36, 80; United Free Church, Pinner, 144; Mrs Sylvia Venis, 86, 117, 121, 139, 147, 155; Mr and Mrs M. Verden, 140-1; Mrs Edna Warrin, 102; Robin Weir, 65; the Rev. P. Wood, 132.

Note

Sequence of pictures

The pictures in this book follow a route beginning in the High Street, and then passing to Marsh Road, West End, Bridge Street, Pinner Green, Pinner Hill, along Uxbridge Road to Hatch End, through Pinner Park and Headstone to East End, Church Lane, Paines Lane and Waxwell Lane. Then the further places of Rayners Lane and North Harrow are treated, followed by topics that are not tied to particular areas. When identifying shops, etc., street numbers have been used, even though these may not be readily visible, to overcome the problem that arises if names or trades change.

Introduction

Come to the centre of Pinner and stand at the junction of the High Street, Bridge Street and Marsh Road. Behind the public garden lies an uncovered stretch of the river Pinn, while opposite, the High Street rises up the low hill on which Pinner originated. This view contains much of Pinner's long history: the church at the top, rebuilt in 1321, and two rows of shops and houses extending downward, added throughout the centuries since.

But this is not the whole of Pinner, nor does it represent all of Pinner's history. Two hundred years ago Pinner was a country village of about seven hundred and fifty people, separated from London by miles of country roads. Now those fields are full of thousands of houses, and the village is part of one of the greatest capital cities in the world, whose centre can be reached in well under an hour by rail or road.

In the last two centuries the population has grown and railways have arrived; new roads have been laid out, work and other activities have changed. These have reshaped Pinner into the place we are familiar with today, and the evidence is still around us.

In 1800 Pinner was a classic rural society. It had a body of gentry that owned large estates, farmers, smallholders, agricultural labourers and a few craftsmen and shopkeepers. The village and parish, extending over 3,782 acres, included the present-day areas of Hatch End, Headstone, North Harrow and Rayners Lane, although the last two were not then in existence. By this time Pinner was effectively separate from Harrow, to which it had been largely subordinate for a thousand years. Administration was the responsibility of the Pinner Parish Vestry, a body elected by those who paid local rates levied for the maintenance of the church and the highways and to aid the poor.

The gentry and the farmers were the most influential people in local affairs. They naturally took a prominent role in the Vestry, since rates were charged in proportion to the value of property owned or occupied. In addition they were the chief providers of employment, mostly agricultural work. Agriculture was still the main occupation in Pinner, but the labourer, normally too poor to pay rates, had little influence on local decisions.

There were several mansions: Pinner Hill House; The Lodge in Elm Park Road and Antoneys opposite; West House, The Grove and Pinner Place in Marsh Road; Pinner House in Church Lane; East House and Nower Hill House at East End; Barrow Point House in Paines Lane; The Hall and Dove House in Uxbridge Road.

During the 19th century their owners tended to derive their money from the higher professions or commerce, but did not often keep the house more than one or two generations. They were charitable, conscious of their social obligations, and they promoted, and often fronted, many local organisations. Admiral Spranger of The Hall gave premises to Pinner's first friendly society, The United Brethren, in the 1820s, and was its honorary chairman; William Tooke encouraged several church societies, giving his money and time, and in 1880 provided most of the funds for restoring Pinner Church; Edward Barber fostered anything to do with temperance, and did much to promote cricket in Pinner; George Bird of The Hall and his wife made their gardens available for village fêtes, and in the 20th century their successors, the Nugents, let local people skate on their lake if it froze.

Some of the owners were keen to improve their premises. From about the middle of the 19th century West House and The Hall were drastically altered, Pinner Hill House acquired a new wing, while Barrow Point House was given at least a face lift, if no more. Arthur Tooke of Pinner Hill, a solicitor, and William Barber of Barrow Point, a judge, were enthusiastic builders and between them provided many buildings in the revivalist styles that were so popular then. Tooke's Pinner Hill House, his Pinner Hill Farm and his pair of Gothic cottages for estate workers in Uxbridge Road (now nos 546-8) still remain, but the only substantial Barber building still to be seen is Elthorne Gate at the top of the High Street, built as the *Cocoa Tree Temperance Tavern* in 1878.

Every mansion was surrounded by beautifully laid out gardens, full of flowers and ornamental trees, especially Scots pines. Even today the sites of many of these vanished mansions are marked by a cluster of surviving tall trees. Through the grounds of The Hall, The Grove and The Towers ran the River Pinn, and in each place it was widened and a tiny island formed in the middle. Only the island at The Towers remains, visible in the river just north of Eastcote Road.

The larger estates used most of their land as farms, which, together with the upkeep of the house, gardens and carriages, meant that the owners were considerable employers of both male and female labour. The 19th century was the high point of these establishments. Most of them survived into the 20th century, having sold most of their farmland to other farmers or to housing developers, but in the 1920s they rapidly faded away, victims of the Depression and a changed society in which they were unable to find servants.

There are no privately occupied grand mansions in Pinner now, though there are plenty of smaller choice residences. The grounds of Pinner Hill House have become a golf course, using the mansion as a club house. The grounds of West House have been the Memorial Park since the Second World War, and the house, though so reduced as to be hardly recognisable, is set to be enlarged and become a museum. The garden of Pinner House in Church Lane has been developed, whilst the house itself has become the core of sheltered housing. The other houses have been demolished and their remaining grounds developed for housing. The Grove, The Lodge, Antoneys and Dove House were replaced by large groups of flats; The Hall, Pinner Place and The Towers by more mixed housing. In nearly every case stately trees from the old gardens have been left in place, which enliven the scene and remind us of what was once there.

The system of farming in Pinner changed radically at the start of the 19th century. Though the large old farms—such as Pinner Park, Headstone Manor, Woodhall Farm, Pinnerwood Farm and Oxhey Lane—stayed as before, the common-land of Pinner and the great fields in the south, which had once been farmed by everyone in common, were privatised by Act of Parliament in 1803. New farms were established—Mill Farm in Pinner Hill Road on what had been the common, and in the southern fields, Downs Farm in Cannon Lane and Daniel Hill's farm in Rayners Lane. Downs had a farmhouse, but Hill, who lived at Church Farm near St John's Church, built only a set of workers' cottages with barns and sheds, where Buckingham School now stands. One family who lived in them for half the 19th century was named Rayner, and the lane took its name from these humble people.

Little physical evidence remains of the houses in which the poorest people of Pinner lived. Low wages meant that the average labourer could not afford much rent, so his accommodation was poor, provided either by the subdivision of older timber-framed houses come down in the world, or in purpose-built cottages, cramped and meanly built of boarding and plaster. While some of the former have survived—Orchard Cottage in Waxwell Lane was once much subdivided for this purpose—the other sort were too flimsy to endure long, and the last one in Pinner, 23 Bridge Street, was pulled down in 1989. Like several others, this one had been built in the early 19th century when the pressure of population outran the supply of adaptable older houses, and, like this one, were usually put up on small roadside plots. Many of them were lived in until the Second World War.

Brick was not used for the cheapest houses until the 1830s. Usually they had a plain front, a main room plus scullery downstairs, and two bedrooms above. Many of those in Pinner represented an investment, probably for their old age, by local artisans and craftsmen, who bought a small single or double plot and engaged local tradesmen to do the building. This is the sort of cottage that survives, usually enlarged by rear extensions, and often regarded as desirable these days. There are examples in Waxwell Lane, Camden Row at Pinner Green and Eastcote Road.

By 1841 the population of Pinner had nearly doubled, reaching 1,331 in 1841. It remained static for the next 10 years but by 1861 had leapt to 1,849 and by a similar amount to 2,382 in 1871.

The London and Birmingham Railway crossed the north-east of Pinner in 1837, and a station named Pinner was opened in 1842. After several interim changes it was renamed Hatch End in 1948. There were only a couple of farms in the vicinity at first but, with encouragement from the railway, a new estate of well-to-do villas, called Woodridings, was built nearby in 1855. It was an isolated estate and its residents were Pinner's first commuters, using the train to Euston. In the same year the Commercial Travellers' School transferred to Hatch End, adding two or three hundred more souls in an enclave confined to the school buildings and grounds.

Transport, education, a larger population and an increased proportion of affluent people all combined to alter the economy of Pinner. Local farmers, responding to the metropolitan demand for dairy produce and for hay to feed the horses drawing London traffic, needed fewer workers—in 1851 about forty per cent of the working population of Pinner was engaged in agriculture or related occupations, but only some 15 per cent by 1881. On the other hand, there was a growing demand for domestic servants, gardeners, grooms (who in 1881 made up the largest occupational group at 30 per cent), shop workers and men in the building trades.

The High Street was becoming a shopping street. There was perhaps a handful of shops in Pinner at the start of the 19th century: baker, butcher, shoemaker, tailor and general provisions. More people needed more shops and additional butchers, bakers and cobblers appeared. As the century progressed, the range of goods widened and specialised shops dealt with them—the grocer, greengrocer, dairy, fishmonger, hardware store, stationer, chemist, confectioner—and shops of this sort appeared in Pinner High Street.

A school to cater for most of the local children had been founded in 1844, backed by the vicar and other worthies and run by the National Society. A Methodist Chapel was established in Chapel Lane in 1844, having met in nearby private premises for several years previously, and in 1859 a Baptist Chapel was built alongside—these account for the name of the lane.

All three denominations organised general support and recreational clubs or societies, such as boys' clubs and girls' clubs, mothers' meetings and Bible classes. Financial and practical help was usually forthcoming from the more wealthy residents, who felt a duty to help with the improvement of the less fortunate. At various times there was a Young Men's Institute, a Working Men's Club and the Church Lads' Brigade. There were occasional sewing and gardening classes, discussion groups, Sunday School treats and visiting lecturers, some with lantern slides. A brass band flourished for many years. Penny Readings, concerts and amateur dramatics were occasionally organised and featured local enthusiasts, from the middle-class Penningtons of the Manor House in Waxwell Lane and the Rowland-Browns of Oxhey Grove, to John Lee, the butcher whose name is still engraved in the frontage of 7 High Street, William Clarke the coal merchant and, quite frequently, the vicar. It was a pattern that continued through most of the 20th century as well.

Sport as an organised activity emerged at local as well as national level during this period. Cricket of some sort was played before Edward Barber founded the cricket club in 1878. There were rugby football fixtures against other Middlesex teams in the 1880s, though they seem to have lost popularity after the soccer club was founded in 1892. It was not long before the soccer club was able to field two teams, in colours red and black.

Since then many other sports clubs have flourished—bowls and tennis in particular. Village sports used to feature, but it is not known whether they took place regularly or only at times of national celebration, such as jubilees and coronations.

The arrival of the Metropolitan Railway in 1885 was very significant for Pinner, producing much more two-way contact between it and the City. On the one hand it enabled many more people, better educated by now, to take work in London, and school records show that the headmaster was well aware of this. He gave his best pupils special lessons to fit them to pass the necessary tests for clerical work, an opportunity of which their parents could not have dreamed. On the other hand it meant that many more Londoners could buy a home in the country. The main-line railway through Hatch End, now part of the London & North Western, set up an omnibus service to encourage residents nearer the centre of Pinner to use its service. It operated for 29 years as the only bus service in Pinner, with one vehicle and one driver only. By 1914 motor buses on new routes had made it redundant.

Nowadays it is difficult to envisage the centre of Pinner minus the railway bridge passing over Marsh Road and Chapel Lane. There was considerable displacement to make way for it. In Chapel Lane several cottages at the Bridge Street end had to go, including the former workhouse behind them, which had been converted into several homes. The Baptist Chapel, only a quarter of a century old, was demolished and rebuilt at the corner of Cecil Park, where, several decades later, it became Pinner's first synagogue. About four cottages in Marsh Road went to make way for the approach to the station, as well as Marsh Farm, whose site lies under the tracks. On the opposite side of the road *The George*, the old timber-framed public house, was pulled down and replaced by the present brick building.

The rising demand for houses from Londoners tempted local landowners of all sorts. At first it was moderately sized plots in streets near the centre of Pinner that were offered for sale by farmers; for example, along the north-east side of Elm Park Road and at the junction of Pinner Road with Marsh Road and Nower Hill. The Rummens family at The Grove moved away and sold off some roadside plots along Marsh Road and Eastcote Road. All these plots sprouted houses.

A large estate, William Barber's Barrow Point, was offered for development in 1898 by his executors. Close to the centre of Pinner, it reached from Paines Lane to Waxwell and Love Lanes. These frontages, together with three whole new streets, Avenue Road, Leighton Avenue and Barrow Point Avenue, were laid out and developed over the next twenty years or so. At Hatch End, far from the centre but close to the main-line station, a huge tract of farmland was sold in 1891 and over some thirty years was turned into the Royston Park Estate. In 1902 the Metropolitan Railway began building Cecil Park on land it owned as a result of its purchases for the railway line. It was its first venture of the kind.

In the 20 years after 1871 the population rose by almost two hundred a decade, rising by over six hundred in the final 10 years of the century. By 1911 its had more than doubled from 3,366 to 7,103. In the late 1870s shops spread beyond the High Street to a few purpose-built premises at the corner of Bridge Street and Chapel Lane.

The built-up parts of Pinner prefigured the later areas, which would see themselves as separate. As well as Hatch End, North Harrow had begun to appear as a new residential area before the First World War, in anticipation of the arrival of North Harrow Station in 1915, and parts of Headstone Manor were already being built upon as Harrow spread. By the end of the war there were several stations in Pinner: Pinner, North Harrow and Rayners Lane (opened 1906), all on branches of the Metropolitan Line, plus Hatch End Station and Headstone Lane Station, just outside Pinner, both on the main line.

The First World War touched the villages of England as no other conflict had before. Whereas a few young men from Pinner (of whom Thomas Ellement was the most well-known) had volunteered for the Boer Wars, this war required not only volunteers, but conscripts. It is thought that about four hundred altogether went from Pinner, but their exact number, including the wounded and killed, is not known. At home there were shortages of food as well as manpower. Local effort included work circles and sewing-bees to make 'comforts' for the troops, and fund-raising fêtes were held at some of the big houses. Pinner Place in Marsh Road, being then vacant, was taken over as a convalescent hospital for war-wounded, who sometimes found themselves welcomed into local homes. It is said that North Harrow Station (opened 1915) had a female station master who lived in Bridge Street, though this cannot be verified. The War Memorial at the top of the High Street was unveiled in 1921 and has been the focus of Remembrance services ever since.

After the war Pinner's appearance outside of the centre was completely changed by the inter-war development of London, producing suburbs of a somewhat different character. The population in 1921 reached 9,462.

The Metropolitan Railway had surplus land to develop in other areas, and in 1915 conceived a series of estates full of comfortable new houses in semi-rural surroundings and with easy access to 'real' countryside, with a guidebook titled 'Metroland'. The Cecil Park Estate was the precursor of them all. The post-war campaign was very successful. The publicity perpetuated the image of Pinner, promulgated in the earliest developments in the 19th century, as a pretty country village of tree-filled lanes, whose dwellings were of good quality.

The Metropolitan Railway's property company attempted to replicate the Metroland style just north of Rayners Lane Station. Here it built a new estate, which it called Harrow Garden Village, hoping (vainly) to get the name of the station changed to the same. The layout, from several roads east of Imperial Drive to Rayners Lane, had the same qualities as the other Metroland estates—generously sized houses, grass verges, closes, houses angled across corners, and it incorporated many of the old trees, especially in Rayners Lane itself.

However, conditions had changed. Houses were needed in numbers greater than had hitherto been conceived, and much more speedily. The newer farms of south Pinner, where the land was more open than elsewhere, with few, and by now absentee, owners, were ideal for rapid housing development. Companies geared to laying out and constructing estates on a large scale were ready. Apart from Harrow Garden

Village, the new roads were lined rather more closely with houses, mostly semi-detached, built to slightly less generous specifications. North of Rayners Lane Station the most prolific firm was Cutlers Ltd, a local one that had begun before the First World War with the 'county' roads at North Harrow, north of Pinner Road. It had many associated firms belonging to members of the Cutler family. South of Rayners Lane Station most of the land in Pinner was acquired by Thomas Nash Ltd, a larger firm that also built in Kenton and Eastcote. Nash had carpentry works at Wealdstone, a little railed system to run materials around the sites and its own estate offices with fleets of cars to take buyers over unmade roads. Its houses were slightly smaller and cheaper than those north of the railway, mostly arranged in terraces of three to six, but the chief roads still had grass verges and all roads were lined with trees.

Into south Pinner went new schools, churches, recreation grounds, shops, rather grand public houses and splendid cinemas, while Bridge Street was virtually rebuilt as the shopping street of the centre. The whole was too large an inhabited area to be covered by the name of Pinner, and the names of the stations serving it came to designate new neighbourhoods. North Harrow and Rayners Lane Stations gave rapid access to Baker Street Station and to the heart of the City. They were good selling points. Thus Pinner became home to a new influx of residents, from London and from other parts of the United Kingdom. Its origins and age group were fairly homogeneous. In return for the life of commuters, families had new homes with all modern conveniences, a garden to tend and play in, sports facilities for the energetic, plenty of other recreational societies, shops, church, cinema and neighbours of similar age, lifestyle and interests—and everything within a moderate radius. For a short time, until the next band of suburbia appeared, country fields were within easy reach.

Lucky Pinner! It was at just this period that plans were being made to establish a belt of land free from houses—a green belt—around London, to interpose a break in the extent of built-up area. It would cover northern Pinner, incorporating the golf course on the hill and Pinnerwood Farm, Oxhey Lane Farm and then eastwards into Harrow Weald and beyond. In 1930 Pinner Park Farm, known as Hall's Farm, had already been preserved as open space by the local council. All of this added together ensured that Pinner would not become wholly suburban, but would keep something different in its character. The residents' appreciation of these values led them to form the Pinner Association in 1932, an amenity society that has continued to guard and promote what is good about the neighbourhood.

The Great Depression of the 1930s did not stem the growth of Pinner. There was no shortage of men to do the building work, while house prices were moderated by the economic difficulties. The area seemed full when the Second World War broke out. The men, and many women, disappeared on military service more completely than in 1914, and the war effort demanded much more of everyone else's time. Some involvement was required, for example in Civil Defence, such as Air Raid Precautions, fire-watching, Ambulance Service, Home Guard, Women's Voluntary Service or, for the youth, the Scout and Guide Movements. In the earlier war, Pinner people had watched Zeppelins in the sky; in this one they suffered direct bombing and, whilst it could not compare in intensity with that over other parts of London, many houses were ruined and many people were killed.

The memorial for this war differed from that of the first one. West House and its grounds, ripe for redevelopment—Cutlers Ltd had begun the process of buying it—was purchased by public subscription to be a Memorial Park. It was planned to place a Book of Remembrance in a shrine open to public view. A room in the house was adapted for this purpose, and others were used for community activities, but after many years problems of maintenance led to the demolition of the larger part of the house and subsequently to the removal of the book to the local authority offices. Present plans are for the house to be re-extended and refurbished so that it can be used as a museum and gallery for the William Heath Robinson Trust, and once again house the Book of Remembrance and provide facilities for local affairs. Heath Robinson, who drew ingenious machines that came to be called 'Heath Robinson contraptions' and brought him the nickname 'the gadget king', lived in Wellington Road from 1908-13 and then in Moss Lane until 1918.

Since the last war the rate of movement of people into and out of Pinner has been high, even though many people who grew up here before the Second World War still live here. A large number of residents, or their forebears, have come to live here from all five continents. There is also a loosening of social cohesion within Pinner, the chief agents being the car, television and the employment of married women, though not necessarily in that order. The car has made people very mobile; they need not depend on neighbours or local facilities for friends or leisure activity, but can maintain links and associate with friends and those of like interest further afield. Entertainment in the home provides an alternative not just to the cinema but to local societies as well, while mothers going to work have less need, or time, for day or evening social activity. Children can be taken easily to friends or pastimes in other areas.

From being the status symbol of a minority prior to the war, car ownership was so widely spread by 1990 that not only were streets heavily parked but the streetscape itself began to change as the front gardens and kerbside trees, so desirable and important in the beginning, were converted to hard standing with dropped kerbs to relieve some of the street parking.

Away from the shops the housing stock has been increased by dint of infill or redevelopment. A new house is squeezed into a side or back garden, or one or more large houses with big gardens are demolished and replaced by several smaller houses or flats with reduced amenity space, of which a large part is paved for car parking. The process sometimes gives rise to protest from neighbours, occasionally with success. It is even feared that the overall increase in hard standing will counter the efforts made to control flooding by the Pinn.

In the north of Pinner, those very houses whose spaciousness attracted newcomers a century or more ago are prime candidates for such treatment. Along The Avenue, the pride of the Royston Park Estate, small blocks are steadily filling the gardens or replacing the houses from Uxbridge Road northward. Uxbridge Road suffers in the same way along its length—indeed, Pinner's tallest blocks of flats stand on the site of Dove House. Elsewhere, two former industrial sites became available at the end of the 20th century, namely the old gas works in Eastcote Road and the gas-holder and civic nursery sites at the extreme south of Cannon Lane. They have been quickly filled with houses and flats.

Many of the new dwellings have slightly smaller rooms than before, and the roof space is used for accommodation instead of storage. At the same time there is great demand for houses with more than four bedrooms, plus family room, study, conservatory and, above all, several bathrooms and a hi-tech kitchen. There are some novel expedients, at Rayners Lane, where an additional storey has been added to a block of flats, and in Bridge Street, where the same is being done for a row of offices that replaced the *Red Lion*.

Shopping has changed enormously, especially for shops that sold foodstuffs and household provisions. Small premises that previously sold a defined range of goods such as groceries, hardware or fish, where the customer queued for attention, first became self-service versions of the same, and then huge supermarkets combining the goods of several types of shop and in greater variety, which enabled the car-owning customer to reduce the number of shopping trips. Pinner has five of them. One is planned for North Harrow, but Rayners Lane has never had one, perhaps because parking space is lacking. Although shopkeepers of Asian origin are plenteous in all shopping centres, it is only at Rayners Lane that Asian foodstores abound.

Small shops selling other goods continue, however, and newer ranges of goods, such as home entertainment and mobile phones, and that newcomer to the scene, the charity shop, have helped fill many of those smaller premises made redundant. In addition there are greater numbers of estate agents and, most noticeably, restaurants, cafés and fast-food shops. Eating places have proliferated in all parts of the former Pinner, though the more expensive ones tend to be at Hatch End and the more picturesque in central Pinner. The variety of cuisine offered reflects how the national palate has changed in the last 50 years, the result of both more foreign travel and the arrival of residents from abroad.

The 21st century has brought the arrival of a Sunday farmers' market behind *The Queen's Head* and the occasional take-over of Bridge Street by a French market, while in the last few years shopping streets have acquired a continental look from the tables and chairs put outside cafés, even in the cooler days of spring and autumn. This is especially true of Pinner High Street, which now belies the old meaning of its name as the main shopping street. But it has benefited from the care taken to keep it alive by creating access directly into it from two of the supermarket enclaves.

The Zoroastrian Centre at Rayners Lane is the only surviving example in Pinner of that proud flagship of suburbia, the cinema. The Langham at Pinner and the Embassy at North Harrow were demolished in favour of supermarkets, but the Grosvenor/Odeon/Ace remained, initially as a club until taken over by the Zoroastrians. Rayners Lane also has one of the last inter-war public houses, called 'roadhouses' because they had large car parks. *The Rayners* was saved from redevelopment only by last-minute listing as a building of architectural merit. The other roadhouse,

The Whittington, renamed *The Pinner Arms*, in Whittington Way, is still operating. *The Headstone Hotel* at North Harrow and *The Orange Tree* (formerly *The Bell*, of old foundation) at Pinner Green have gone. Hatch End's early Victorian pub, *The Railway*, one of the few buildings that gave character to its centre, had only the ineffective protection of being locally listed, and down it came a few years ago.

Pinner has many nationally listed buildings, most of them in the High Street or its environs, which distinguish it and add to its desirability. No wonder then that it is not uncommon to round a corner and find the place cluttered with the huge white vans and paraphernalia that indicate the location for a film or advertising shoot. Even the police station is listed and has been filmed.

It is true to say that the name Pinner now conjures a smaller area than its historic one. It does not include Rayners Lane or North Harrow, Headstone or Hatch End, though where the dividing lines lie it is impossible to say. The name of Pinner still has cachet. The High Street and the nexus of ancient streets around it are often called 'the village', and estate agents find the expression a potent attraction to their clients.

I wonder about the future look and composition of Pinner. As someone very conscious of the past, I hope that it keeps those older (unlisted) dwellings and buildings, which lend it grace and distinction outside as well as inside its conservation areas, that the streets do not become channels of flats and town houses standing behind rows of cars instead of greenery, that it keeps its parks, green belt and those small clusters of trees that dignify roads and corners. It ought to be possible to avoid sacrificing these while still being able to fit in new houses and enjoy and adapt to new things.

1 At the left of the rough-surfaced High Street, sometime between 1865 and 1880, butcher John Lee has taken a delivery of so many carcasses that they overlap *The Crown* next door. The grocery shop on his other side was refronted in the 1890s, doing away with the right-hand gable, and the weather-boarded house is now *Friends*. All the shops beyond have been replaced, except for the tallest, which is nos 21-3. On the right, washing is hanging out in the back garden of nos 4-6 (now *The Victory*) which was built over with nos 8-14 in 1880.

2 On the opposite corner to *The Crown* stood the first bank in Pinner, a branch of Woodbridge's bank, founded in Uxbridge in 1791. The Post Office flanks it at the left, where Robert Rowe was postmaster and draper for nearly 30 years from 1871, while the first *Victory*, actually in Marsh Road, creeps in at the right. This little stretch, with two more shops just beyond *The Victory*, was built in 1860.

3 How quiet this scene looks, the clearest view we have of this part before 1878. The house was called Equestrian Villa, perhaps because from 1822 it belonged to Charles Turner and then George Stanbrough, licensees of *The Queen's Head*, both of whom drove the coach to London until about 1840. The right-hand part dates from about 1800 and is still there, minus the balcony and with reopened windows. That on the left looks a good century older, and was replaced in 1878 by *The Cocoa Tree*, which William Barber built as a temperance tavern.

4 A boy and his dog walk happily up the middle of the High Street in 1904, while a horse and cart park on the pavement. All the houses are business premises. The horse and cart are outside Frederick Gurney's Central Stores (grocery and off-licence), at nos 38-40, and are probably delivering goods. Below Gurneys the horizontal sign by the flagpole of no. 32 apparently refers to 'dinners and teas'. The adjoining white-brick house has been divided into two. On the left a huge wagon is up-ended outside Beaumont's (no. 27), the wheelwright, whose family came there in the late 18th century. There is a tailor in the house with the 'Dye Works' sign adjoining *The Queen's Head*.

5 This slightly later view shows more of the top of the High Street. Again there is pavement parking at the right, this time outside *The Hand in Hand*, which sells Wellers ales. Above it is Saich the saddler's tiny cottage, and then two or three shops, as far as Ashby's building yard, left of which is Piercy's butcher's shop. At the left the awning over *The Cocoa Tree* proclaims it as a temperance hotel. The furthest shop on this side is Hall's the chemist, whose big lamp survives. Below it is Thomas Bros, retail drapers, and then Hedges' bakery, both of them now Pizza Express. A very faded sign perched on the wooden bar of *The Queen's Head* advertises garage facilities.

6 The 'town tree' outside Piercy's was already an old pollarded elm when Victoria came to the throne, and it collapsed in 1898 after showing no sign of life for 15 years. As we can see, its successor, already planted, only just escaped being crushed. It was clearly a fine plaything.

7 Taken before 1898, this photograph illustrates just how gnarled the town tree was. Behind is the butcher's shop with perhaps Hotspur Piercy himself at the door. At the right is the old tall slaughterhouse.

8 This picture from about 1910, with two replacement town trees, shows the replacement slaughterhouse, equally high, but with louvred ventilation. It was probably used until the business closed down about 1930. The date 1307 on the house gable has no historical justification.

9 It is hard to believe that the building in this photograph of 1974 was the slaughterhouse, but it is indeed the very same.

10 This pair of tiny Victorian cottages in the High Street never became shops. They were built about 1840 and called Hedges Cottages after William Hedges of East End Farm bought them in 1860. He left them to his son James. They were replaced by no. 42 in 1927.

11 The scrumptious display of Edwardian confectionery in the window of Peters' Bakery at 33 High Street must have caused many a child to plead with mother for a treat when collecting the loaf. The ornamental glazing has gone, alas!

12 The pair of gables at the left are over 21 High Street, now part of Starbucks, and Bishops Walk (once 23). The houses further left were probably 18th century. From left to right the shops had been a bakery, a draper's and an ironmonger's. Now they are closed and notices announcing redevelopment have been fixed to the shuttered windows. At the right, no. 16 has become the White Hart Dining Rooms.

13 In this Edwardian view nos 21-3 are hidden by the new gabled development to which the three previous trades have returned, some with new owners. During the First World War the bakery, under the left gable, was the subject of anti-German attacks, and the German baker changed his name to Wyatt. Below it Kingham's grocery is also enjoying brand new premises. On the extreme right no. 8 is still a private residence, but the three above have become shops: Emery's stationer, photographer and framer; Gurney's oil and cycle shop, with a pram parked outside, and Hotchin's carrier business just past the pram. There is plenty of traffic. The horse bus is parked halfway up on the left and below it, with a lady awaiting her chauffeur, stands a Vauxhall motor car. This version, without a windscreen, was one of only 20 7-9 hp models made in 1903-4, for a price of £200.

14 This was Pinner Post Office from 1900-10, and the telephone exchange from 1908-10. One of the ladies may be Mrs Newman, postmistress from 1903 and daughter of Robert Rowe, the latter having moved the office from 2 High Street. The lad is Charley Greenfield. The shop was converted into Bishops Walk in the late 1970s to serve Bishop's new supermarket, now Marks & Spencer.

15 James Bedford set up his tailor's workshop at 11 High Street in 1839, and so it remained until his son James died in 1912, aged eighty-five. The wooden board reads 'J Bedford Tailor'. Both were also parish clerks. Edwin Ware moved in with old Jimmy to act as clerk in 1909. After Bedford's death in 1912 the weather-boarding in this picture of *c*.1900 was removed, and the little arched Tudor window at the centre of the first floor was rediscovered. The vine at the right is still alive.

Left: **16** James 'Jimmy' Bedford.

Below: **17** Cycling clubs were popular from about 1890 onwards, and this unknown group has taken refreshment at Shirvell's White Hart Dining Rooms. Descours at the left made corsets as well as luggage. Further left are two pretty bay windows of about 1840; the nearer, which has gone, was Bliss's antique shop, while the left one was a confectioner's. The significance of the unfurled Union Jack is unknown. In 1985 the left half of the dining rooms became Barters Walk, giving access to Sainsbury's supermarket.

Above: **18** Here the cycling group is taking it easy in Shirvell's rose-filled back garden—perhaps that is the boss at the left, wearing an apron. The room from which the photograph was taken became the telephone exchange in 1910. Everything has changed since. The garden is now Barters Walk, the way to Sainsbury's, with steps at the left and slope at the right. The wagons in the railway sidings at the rear, and the brick railway shed, have given way to the supermarket and car parks. A public passageway now runs through the side of Hotchin's garden, in line with the garden gate.

Right: **19** The old *Hand in Hand* and buildings above it were demolished in 1933, to be replaced by Grange Court and 44-54 High Street. That part of Grange Court that turns into the newly created Grange Gardens at the left is rising here, with the help of an enormously long one-piece wooden ladder. The old town tree replacement is doing well.

20 The true nature of 18-24 High Street, built about 1800-20, was revealed when fake timbering was fixed to the upper floor sometime between 1928 and 1934. A blind window had to be levelled first. The delivery bike at the right belongs to Waterhouse, the butcher at no. 18; no. 20 was an electrician's shop although there seems to be a lady's dress on display; Mrs Brown's café is at 22 and Mrs Woodman's sweet shop at 24. Nos 28-30, festooned with tobacco adverts, are Stait's tobacconist, which moved to 8 Bridge Street in 1935. It has an automatic chocolate-vending machine by the door. The car is a British registered U.S.A. model, possibly a 1920s Chevrolet.

21 Four of Woodman's five shops squeeze into this picture. The gardening firm began at no. 21 when Mrs Woodman took over a bankrupt corn chandler's in 1891. No. 19 was added in 1924, 25 in 1935, and 15 in 1938. The family sold the firm in 1972, after which no. 23 was acquired, but the business closed suddenly in February 1975, about the time this picture was taken.

Above: **22** Woodman's staff pose with one of his vans in the shop's outbuildings behind the High Street, probably in the late 1940s. There was a nursery and show garden at Cuckoo Hill, where Nursery Road is now.

Right: **23** The space behind nos 21-3, seen here, was also used to grow plants. In 1972 the new owner opened a garden centre extending down to the car park in Love Lane.

24 This is Cutmore's clothes shop in February 1997, closing after more than 60 years. It began under that name at no. 17, the right-hand part, in 1934, and expanded into no. 15 after Woodman's moved out in 1969.

25 Here we are in Elm Park Road about 1905, looking down Bridge Street. The corner of the Police Station is visible at the left, and beyond it is *The Oddfellows Arms*, and probably the glasshouses of John How, nurseryman. Dears Farm at the left looks sweetly rural. The postcard's caption 'Pinner Hill' is wrong.

26 Dears Farm was demolished in 1935 to be replaced by the Langham Cinema, a nice example of Art Deco with a tiled façade of cream with green banding and an elegantly lettered café at the left. During this week in 1947 it is showing John Mills in 'So Well Remembered' and an old Laurel and Hardy film. The shops at the right stand on Dears garden and still have the bricked-in ground floor of wartime. A supermarket replaced the cinema in the 1980s.

27 Here is another drastically different view of Bridge Street, a little lower down, taken in 1923. Shops nos 53-61 Bridge Street are here now. The centre cottages, still inhabited, probably date from the 18th century and are made of brick, timber and plaster. William Hedges bought them in 1852 and left them to his son George. At the back he built five brick cottages and left them to his son Henry. The detached cottage at the right, named 'The Cottage', is late Victorian.

28 Some people will still remember the vegetable stall in Bridge Street, next to the undertaker, which hid an old cottage (no. 23) at the back. This last gap in the street frontage was filled by a new building in 1989. The view dates from 1974, a few years before Bishop's moved to the new store behind the High Street, which later became Marks & Spencer's first all-food store.

29 The cottage at the back had formed the end of a row of three timber-and-plaster cottages (nos 19-23) built by carpenter Thomas Trevethan in 1806. There were farriers here for 50 years until 1926 and it must have been the last of them, Henry Botten, who made the pretty ironwork over the door, which reads 'H Botten'. After that it was used as Richens' coal office. The last survivor of the row, it came down in 1989.

30 In Bridge Street all eyes are on the fire engine, with volunteer firemen aboard, near the junction with Love Lane about 1910. The Victorian house at the right hides *The Red Lion* and part of the fire station shed at the corner with Love Lane. The shops at the back were built about 1908-9; the Midland Bank at the right has been there from the beginning. The left-hand shops, with typical projecting windows, date from 1872. The nearest shop was Taylor & Pendry's saddlers, and the canopy shades George Hedges' butcher shop. A photographic business operates round the back.

31 It is hard to recognise this as Bridge Street about 1930. The large house is Bridge House, the home of Charles Woodbridge, who had built it about 1850, almost to the edge of the pavement. *The Red Lion* is hidden between it and the fire station to its left, while at the back are the shops curving round to Love Lane. The house went in 1932 (there is now a bus stop outside the front door), at an uncertain date the fire station did too, but *The Red Lion* lasted until 1962.

32 Patrons pose for the camera outside *The Red Lion* at the beginning of the 20th century, when Henry Dyer was licensee. In 1875 this building replaced the earlier *Red Lion*, whose first licensee was probably Francis Barrett in 1727.

33 An open-top 140b bus approaches *The Red Lion* in 1926. The upper part of Bridge Street has not changed yet. The house at the distant left is Dears Farm.

34 Brewster's newsagents, previously Beaumont's, stood at the corner of Chapel Lane and Bridge Street, one of the row built by Ellement in 1872. The window is full of cards and postcards; *The Morning Post*, *Tribune* and *Telegraph* are advertised, and the windowsills are gay with potted flowers. The barely visible tablet beside the right upper window reads 'Bridge Place 1872', and when this shop was knocked down in 1930s for Woolworth's it was put on the front of no. 21. The photo probably dates from the early 20th century.

35 From time to time the Pinn overflows and property at the corner of Bridge Street and Chapel Lane is particularly vulnerable to inundation. This was taken on 8 May 1988 when Pinner was flooded seriously—twice in the same day.

36 These cottages at the corner of Chapel Lane opposite Woolworth's, photographed in 1969, were built in the 1840s. The only survivors of several along here, they were enlarged into Chapel Lane Chambers in the later 1980s. A proposal in 1890 to build the fire engine shed at the left came to naught.

37 Charles Woodbridge built these three brick-and-timber cottages to the left of Chapel Lane Chambers between 1842 and 1855—they were very close to the edge of the Pinn. The left-hand one was always a shoemaker's shop. The photograph was taken in 1936, six years before demolition without replacement.

38 How different this view of Chapel Lane must have looked before the intrusion of the railway bridge. The cottage dated from about 1600 and was one of those subdivided for cheap letting, in this case into three. The picture is *c.*1900. Round the corner beyond the bridge, two chapels and more than half a dozen small houses, plus another six out of shot in the left foreground, give the lie to the lonely mood.

Right: **39** Right opposite the previously pictured cottages stood this mid-19th-century one where James and Catherine Langthorn lived. They moved out in 1885 when the railway embankment was built across the spot. There are flower boxes at the windows and a birdcage hanging by the door.

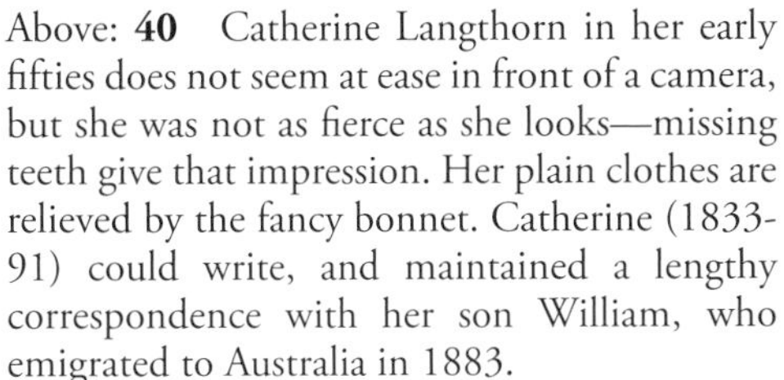

Above: **40** Catherine Langthorn in her early fifties does not seem at ease in front of a camera, but she was not as fierce as she looks—missing teeth give that impression. Her plain clothes are relieved by the fancy bonnet. Catherine (1833-91) could write, and maintained a lengthy correspondence with her son William, who emigrated to Australia in 1883.

Right: **41** James Langthorn's whiskers have disarranged his bow tie. His best clothes look thick and warm, the top coat drawn back to show off the watch on a chain. James (1836-94) was an agricultural labourer and, unlike his wife, he could not write. All the same he has an air of confidence. These last three photographs were sent to William in Australia.

42 Marsh Road at the foot of Station Approach about 1974. The tiled building was originally a cottage, probably dating from the 1840s. John Gurney added three shops at the left about 1860, though the furthest, the first *Victory*, has gone. All these, and the two kiosks, were demolished in 1985 when Sainsbury's was built.

43 This also went in 1985. Kiosks like this appeared beside stations in the 1930s, usually to accommodate estate agents and coal merchants. This had become the Pinner Stamp Shop by the early 1960s.

44 The whole bulldozed site beside Station Approach in May 1985, with the minicab office still at bay.

45 In 1885 the railway tracks behind the minicab office obliterated Marsh Farm, whose history went back hundreds of years. This drawing of 1885 shows a picturesque 16th- or 17th-century farmhouse, with a lean-to pigeon loft at the left, and beside that a granary. At the front left stands a barn.

46 Carriages are lined up outside *The George* around 1900. The stable just fits between it and the railway embankment. The pub was rebuilt in 1889, after all the dislocation of constructing the embankment for the Metropolitan Line to Northwood Hills was over.

47 A carriage departs from the original *George*, which was in business during the 1740s. No railway embankment looms because the pub was knocked down ahead of its construction. This picture was painted about 1880.

48 These five cottages, sketched before demolition in 1885, were converted from the workhouse after the Hendon Poor Law Union took over management of the Pinner poor in 1834. They were built in 1785 near *The George* but on the further side of the Pinn, as the bridge shows.

49 The railway embankment sweeps down to a row of elms, which gave their name to a house demolished *c.*1910 to make way for 100-114 Marsh Road. Across the road the stable of *The George* peeps out to the right. Marsh Cottages at the left have been replaced by Monument House.

50 The five Marsh Cottages were gradually pulled down between 1960 and 1980 and replaced by the Bridge Garage. This is the middle cottage, the last to go, photographed in 1974. At the left are the backs of houses in West End Avenue.

51 Here is the Bridge Garage in 1986, with a hoarding still masking the site of the last cottage. Monument House covered the lot in 1986.

52 Marsh Road does not have that name for nothing—the flooding of 1988 even marooned a car in School Lane.

53 Nos 86-98 Marsh Road were new in this picture of 1915. The Baptist Chapel at the corner of Cecil Park replaced the one demolished in Chapel Lane in 1885. By 1915 it was the Pinner Men's Club. In 1941 it became Pinner Synagogue, and was rebuilt in 1981, requiring the removal of the nearest house. The Pinn flows behind the trees at the left, though West End Avenue has bridged it where the road bends.

54 The bridge in this summer scene of *c.*1900 is in Eastcote Road, by today's Holwell Place. The banks on the nearer side belong to Pinner Place, one of Pinner's mansions, while on the other side of the bridge the Pinn flows through the grounds of another, The Grove. The sluice was used to regulate the flow of the stream.

Above: **55** John Mayall, court photographer, sold The Grove to Francis Rummens in 1865. Set in extensive grounds with the Pinn running through, it lay behind the corner of Marsh Road and Eastcote Road. From this west side of the house, the path runs left to the entrance in Marsh Road. The photo dates from about 1880.

Left: **56** Francis Rummens was a railway contractor, the Great Central Railway providing a good deal of his business. In 1874 he added Canons Farm to his estate and at one time it seemed he was hoping that the course of the Metropolitan Railway would run across it.

Right: **57** Elinor Rummens was the younger daughter of Francis. Here she is, smart and curled, in 1878, at the age of twenty-two. It was Elinor who painted the picture of the old *George*.

Below: **58** Within the grounds of the Grove the Pinn was widened, as is clear from this photo of the 1880s. A little boat is moored against the left bank. The house is on the same side of the stream, and Eastcote Road or Cannon Lane is some distance over to the right.

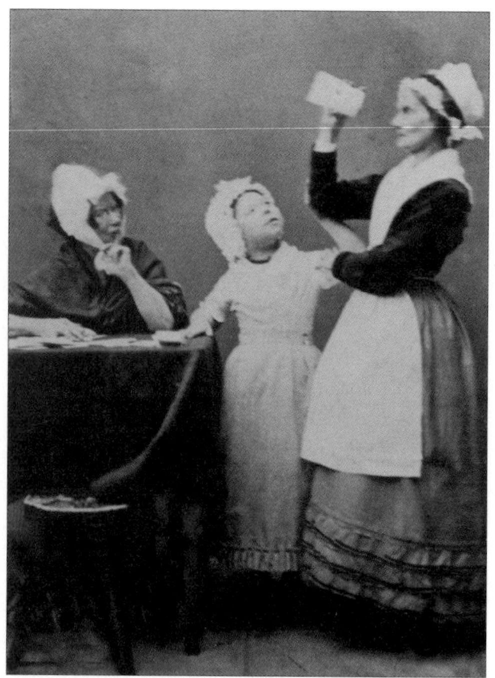

Right: **59** Rummens' daughter Katherine suffered from dwarfism and was about thirty years old when this photo was taken, probably in 1878, depicting her engaged with two of the servants, Mrs McCrae, left, and Mrs Hadlow, right. Like her sister, she painted local scenes.

Left: **60** Henry Hawkins was Rummens' bailiff, and managed Canons Farm for him.

Right: **61** These lambs are probably being fed at Canons Farm. The house would have stood in the slip-road in front of the shops near Hereford Gardens, and the taller barn in this picture is probably the one that still stands behind the shops.

62 This picture, taken in 1935 or 1936, shows Cannon Lane at a significant time. The houses on the left, or west, side, arrived about 1930, whilst the shops at the right were built in 1935. Whittington Way has yet to be fully broken through. Canons Farm is in the middle distance, and the trees beyond conceal houses on each side of the road. Apart from the one with the lambs, this is the only picture of Canons Farm, demolished in 1937, to come to light.

63 The tablet on this bridge carrying Cannon Lane tells that it was rebuilt in 1728 by Lady Hunsdon, who owned the land all around. This 1928 photo shows a haystack on the further side of Cannon Lane that belonged to Canons Farm, just out of the picture on the left. Since then the lane has filled with houses and Hereford Gardens runs in at the left. The bridge has been rebuilt and the tablet re-affixed to the parapet at the west side of Cannon Lane.

64 A man stands beside a telegraph pole in the half-flooded Eastcote Road, 1910. The camera looks south from West End Lane to where the Pinn passes underneath the road, which then turns left. Beyond the bridge is the single-storey lodge to The Towers, sporting a 'For Sale' sign. It is now covered by Lloyd Court. The leftward-stretching row of trees marks the line of the Pinn, on the other side of which Lyncroft Avenue was later made. Behind that is the lodge to Canon Croft, now Ellement Close.

65 At The Towers lived Arthur and Agnes Marshall, he a businessman and she a celebrity cook. They pause at the main entrance in their Panhard one day in 1904, while the manservant waits to bring over the travel rugs. Arthur sits beside the chauffeur, but it is not clear which of the ladies, hats tied down with scarves, is Agnes.

66 Arthur was once Chairman of Pinner Gas Company in Eastcote Road. All that remained when this picture was taken in 1986 were sheds converted to storage for North Thames Gas. The site was redeveloped in 2000 for luxury flats, called 40 Eastcote Road. The corner wall of purple bricks around the telephone box is still there.

67 The North Thames Gas office block, with the sheds at its right and Oak Cottages at its left, ended as a Scientific Service Station. It was demolished for the flats.

68 In West End Lane, around Dickson Fold, there used to be a clutch of old cottages made of brick, or just timber and plaster, which lasted until about 1956. They were let to labourers and usually contained a living room and scullery downstairs, plus two bedrooms above. Lavatories were at the end of the gardens. These three, with the row close behind, date from the early 19th century. West End Lane is at the left.

69 This was the rear row of cottages, with weather-boarded end wall and brick ground floor. West End Lane is at the right. Both rows stood on the site of 16-17 Dickson Fold.

70 Box Cottage stood across the end of the two rows, masking them and facing onto West End Lane. It would have been about 1850 in date.

71 Nowadays you will find that 1-3 West End Cottages has replaced this pair, known as West House Cottages. Apparently just timber and plaster, they may have dated from the late 18th century.

72 West House had been the mansion of West End. The last private owners left before the Second World War and it was given over to Civil Defence services. Afterwards, house and grounds were bought to be a Memorial Park. This picture probably dates from about that time, to judge by the anti-blast wall at the left, and the unkempt condition of the garden.

73 This romantic scene is of the house servants enjoying the facilities while the owner, John Hogg, was away. Most of West House was 19th-century in date. The whole of the creeper-clad section, and the part with the right-hand balcony, has gone.

Above: **74** The owners of West House pose in the garden about 1907, possibly near one of the two remaining great oak trees. Sydney Hogg is at the left, in a cap almost as wide as his wife's hat, with son Frank in front of him and son Edward in front of Frances, who had inherited the house from her father William Dickson. The dog may be one of those whose memorial stone can still be found in the garden.

Right: **75** An inattentive Edward Hogg stands with his sister Dorothy beside the lake at West House about 1906.

76 In 1873 William Dickson had let West House to Nelson Ward, grandson of Admiral Lord Nelson and Lady Hamilton. Nelson Ward, son of the Admiral's daughter Horatia, is shown below. His wife Jessie Bird, from The Hall, Pinner, is shown at the left.

77 Nelson and Jessie's eight children were the great-grandchildren of Admiral Nelson. Here are young Nelson, their eldest son, who later in life had the word 'adopted' on Horatia's tomb altered to 'beloved', and their last child Maurice, taken about 1875.

78 Mary and Catherine were the Wards' second pair of twins, born in 1869.

79 Agnes, last but one, was born in 1870. She married Cameron Dickson, son of William, and their son William Dickson became a Marshal of the Air Force. All the photographs on this page were taken by John Mayall, formerly of The Grove.

80 The remnant of West House can be compared with the picture showing the anti-blast wall. The huge swamp cypress tree in front of it appears in both, and is reckoned to date from the mid-19th century. Conversion to a museum has involved the demolition of the oldest part, the single-storey stable remnant, at the end of 2006, but it is likely to be rebuilt.

81 It was at first intended to place the Book of Remembrance in a shrine in the park, and this was the design proposed by local architect Harold Greenwood. It did not come to fruition.

82 Westbury Lodge was a late-19th-century house at the corner of Chapel Lane and West End Lane. The gardens were often opened to the public in springtime and the magnolia tree at the right of the picture survived when the house was demolished for the Westbury Lodge Estate in the 1970s.

83 The sweet-looking Poplar Cottage stood in West End Lane, behind the present no. 83, from the late 16th century until 1939.

84 The lettering on the milk cart speaks for itself, though neither date nor location is known. The Victorian West End Farmhouse and some of its outbuildings still stand beside West Lodge School. The milkman's name is said to be Sid Messenger.

85 Here is the brand new replacement *Bell* at Pinner Green in 1930, before it is fully finished—the name and other signage has not yet been put up, and the post is waiting for its hanging sign of a bell. In 1999 the name was changed to *The Orange Tree*, but in 2005 it was replaced by a block of flats.

86 A view from the other direction about 1906 has the earlier *Bell* at the right. The cottages to the left, then called Belle Vue, are still there as Pinner Green. James Garwood's family is standing outside no. 6, and James was probably the Jim who wrote and sent the postcard of this view.

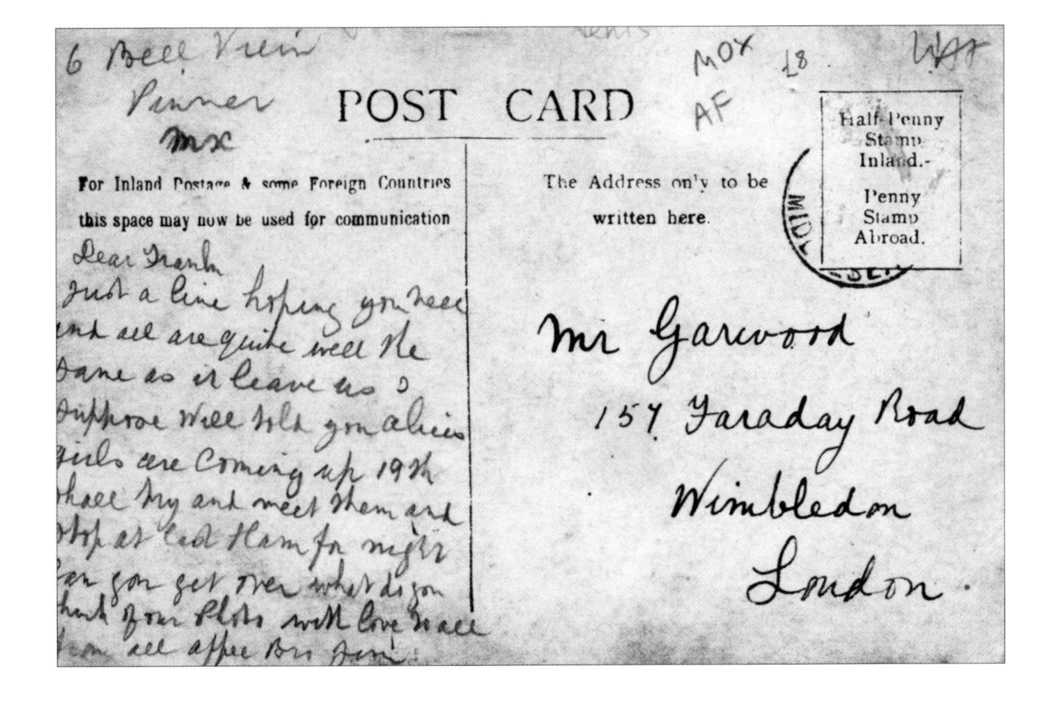

6 Bell View
Pinner
Mx

POST CARD

For Inland Postage & some Foreign Countries this space may now be used for communication

Dear Frank
Just a line hoping you and
all are quite well the
same as it leave us I
suppose Will told you Alice's
girls are coming up 19th
shall try and meet them and
stop at Ced Ham for night
can you get over what do you
think of our plots with love to all
from all affec Bro Jim

The Address only to be written here.

Half-Penny Stamp Inland.- Penny Stamp Abroad.

Mr Garwood
157 Faraday Road
Wimbledon
London.

87 This is Rickmansworth Road, looking west, about a century ago. The nearer cottages are a row of six built in 1830 and were known as Barter's Cottages by the time they were demolished in 1935. Those beyond were at first a terrace of three, and are still there as a pair, 88 and 92, dating from about 1880, while across the road a surviving terrace is just visible, either 73-83 or 85-95, built by Charles Woodbridge in the 1890s.

88 Though St Edmund's Church in Rickmansworth Road is just outside Pinner, the larger part of its parish is inside. This is the first church, built in 1935. In 1963-4 a lofty new church was added to the left at a right angle to the old one, incorporating the old chancel as the Lady Chapel of the new. The old nave, at the right, became the church hall.

89 This is the only picture so far known of The Nook, a gentleman's residence at the corner of Pinner Hill Road, with its entrance here in Uxbridge Road. Built by Charles Woodbridge in the 1840s, the rather dull house was pulled down in about 1939 and replaced by Montesole Court after the war.

90 The 17th-century miller's house, sitting well back from Pinner Hill Road near the windmill, had been converted into three labourers' cottages. They were called Mill Farm Cottages, and in 1914 Mrs Burch, foreground, and Mrs Furness at the rear, seem happy to be photographed. Hardly lived in after the war, the cottages came down in 1960 to make way for Mill Farm Close.

91 The incongruous tower of Pinner Hill Farm was a largely useless decoration to its attached small stable. Its elegant roof, very decrepit in this 1976 view from the farmyard, was replaced in 1980 by a good copy. During the 1970s the farm premises were used for stabling horses.

92 Here is Pinner Hill Farmhouse in 1976, facing onto its farmyard. In the last quarter-century the farm buildings, including those beside the house, and the tower stable, have been converted into dwellings or offices.

93 During restoration a horse circle was uncovered behind the stable beside the house. When turned by the horse, the mechanism at the centre rotated a rod sunk in the groove crossing the circle at the lower right, which operated a crushing-stone in a building, at this date vestigial, off-camera.

94 Crinolined ladies stroll up to Pinner Hill House in this engraving of 1854, before the present front wing was added by Arthur Tooke in the 1860s.

95 The ornate front door and windows of the new wing are lost in flowers sometime about 1910.

96 Tooke's front-wing projects above the earlier, ivy-covered rear of Pinner Hill House in the silent snow, about 1910.

97 The equine complement of Pinner Hill House was accommodated in these stables, pictured in 1980. The arched doors mark the coach house, and there was lodging for a groom upstairs at the extreme right. All went in the 1990s, except for the small central portion with two blocked upper openings and a bricked-up door. They dated from about 1830, or perhaps a little later.

Left: **98** Alice Helsham-Jones, holding her fourth daughter, Angelet, on her lap, was the owner of Pinner Hill House after her brother William Tooke died in 1884. It was William who had paid for the restoration of St John's Church in 1880.

Right: **99** Arthur Helsham-Jones was Alice's husband. They used to entertain W.S. Gilbert of Grimsdyke at Pinner Hill together.

100 Angelet must be about ten years old as she sits side-saddle on Jess, her pony. The scene is probably not Pinner Hill.

101 Samuel Lammas Dore, second from right, bearded, bought Pinner Hill from the Helsham-Jones's in 1903. He was an industrialist. A few years after he died in 1919 the estate was sold, part of it being turned into the golf course, part into a private estate.

102 The crowd gathers round the luminaries of an international match hosted by Pinner Hill Golf Club in 1956. The players, holding clubs, are (left to right): Trevor Wilkes (in peaked cap and cardigan) and Gary Player for South Africa, Bernard Hunt and John Jacobs for Great Britain. 'Dickie' Warrin, the club captain, stands between Wilkes and Player, and looking over his shoulder is bearded Horace Cutler, later Chairman of the Greater London Council.

103 Antoneys, a small mansion whose history went back to medieval times, looked out over Uxbridge Road near the corner with Elm Park Road. At the time of this painting, *c.*1910, the owner was Sir Frank Ree, general manager to the London and North Western Railway, which passed through Hatch End.

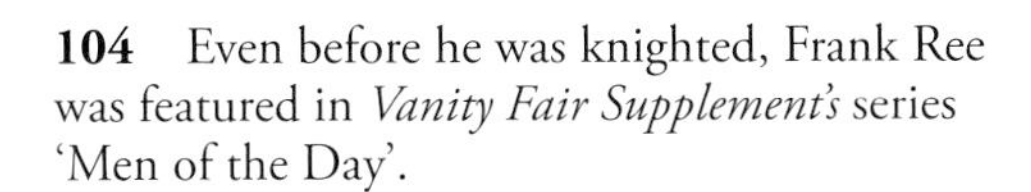

104 Even before he was knighted, Frank Ree was featured in *Vanity Fair Supplement's* series 'Men of the Day'.

105 Sir Frank is discussing things with his gardener (extreme left). The house was demolished in 1952 and the house site, with most of the garden, lies beneath the close and flats at Antoneys.

106 No. 607 Uxbridge Road, pictured in 1980, is all that remains of The Hall estate—a lodge sporting patterned slates and fancy ridge tiles. In front is part of the wall and a gatepost, once topped by a lamp. The lodge was subsequently extended to the left. At the right is Old Hall Drive, which used to lead to the mansion.

107 The Pinn ran through the grounds of The Hall, and the drive crossed it at the point where a lake had been created. This picture of the bridge was taken from an island in the lake during 1928, a year before the lake was drained. A vestige of the bridge remains.

108 George Bird had built houses and churches in Hammersmith, where his father was a brickmaker. He went on to construct roads and sewers in west London, including Kensington Palace Gardens. When he bought The Hall in 1865 he restyled it along Kensington lines. His daughter Jessie, pictured elsewhere, married Nelson Ward.

109 Woodhall Towers was a tremendously ornate folly of a house built by Arthur Tooke in 1863. It was used briefly as a hotel *c.*1930, and here is its courtyard, with the implication of country activities to hand.

110 This close-up of the highest tower, about 1939, reveals its intricate Gothic Revival detail. After demolition in 1962, the stone clock-face found a home in the garden of a member of the Ellement family, which did much work for Tooke and may have been concerned with this building.

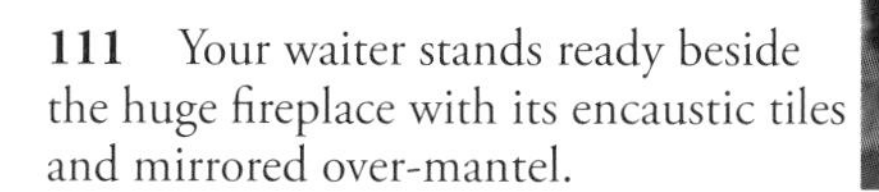

111 Your waiter stands ready beside the huge fireplace with its encaustic tiles and mirrored over-mantel.

112 In 1933 the trees at the right hid Woodhall Towers, while the clump at the end hid Woodhall Farm. The house at the left, 11 Woodhall Drive, was the home of T.L.J. Bentley, who took this and fig.110.

113 Another Bentley photo, taken late one afternoon in 1933, shows where Woodhall Drive dropped and curved beyond Woodhall Farm. The future line of Woodhall Gate appears ahead, and the fields beyond will all too soon be covered by Marsworth Avenue and Evelyn Drive. The hut below left is on the triangular green beside The Link.

114 Aircraft enthusiast Arthur Ord-Hume drastically reconstructed an old Luton Minor G-AFIR in his parents' garden at 24 Evelyn Drive and made his first flight on 1 May 1951, using the field over the hedge in Woodhall Farm for take-off. This is now Langland Drive and Ferndown Close. The estate landlords accused him of lowering the tone of the neighbourhood! Ord-Hume continued all his life to pioneer the design and construction of home-made aircraft.

115 During the 1930s, *The Railway Hotel's* façade was simplified to be more in key with the times. It was one of the very few buildings lending character to the centre of Hatch End, yet it was abruptly flattened for new development late in 2004.

116 Hatch End Station, rebuilt in 1911, is very new in this picture. The name just below the roof is 'Pinner Station' (though the fuller name Pinner & Hatch End had been in use since 1897). There is a glass canopy, and the notice boards have not yet been fixed to the side wall at the right. The street lamps are elegant and a railwayman drives a motorised freight tricycle.

117 Woodridings School flourished from 1898-*c.*1960 in this purpose-built house in Uxbridge Road at the east corner of Altham Road. It was a private school for girls and juniors that had begun, briefly, at Fairholme in The Avenue.

Above: **118** This is the rear façade of the Royal Commercial Travellers' School as seen from the railway. Built as a boarding school in 1855 and opened by the Prince Consort, closure came in 1967, followed by demolition of this building. A supermarket stands there today.

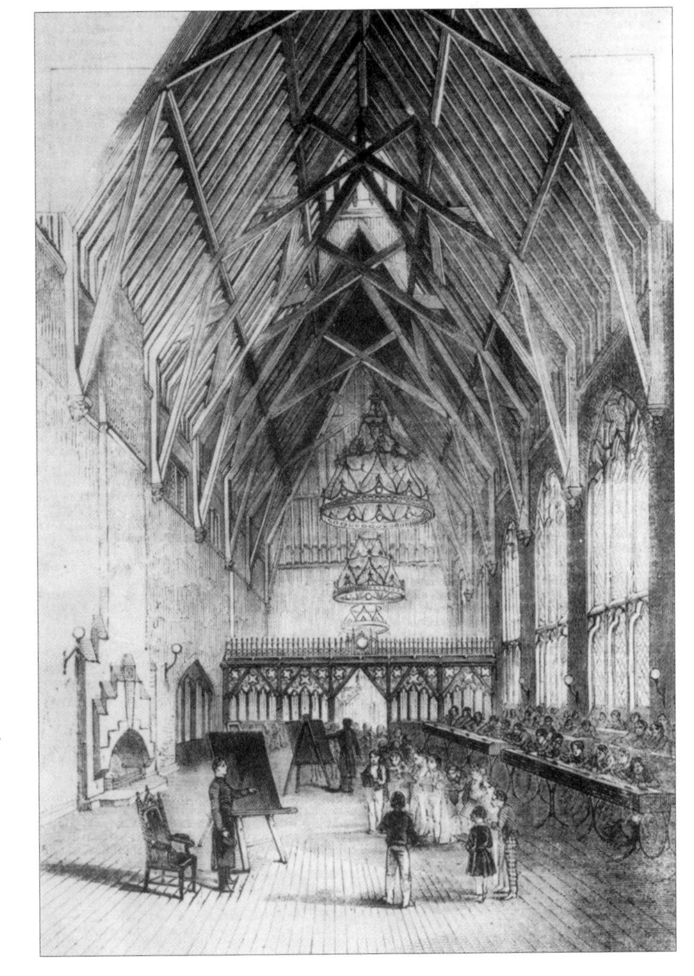

Right: **119** Here is the main school room in 1855, on the upper floor at the rear, beneath the spire. Teaching several classes in one hall was the usual method at that time. In this case proximity may have helped the children keep warm, because that fireplace would not have given out much heat.

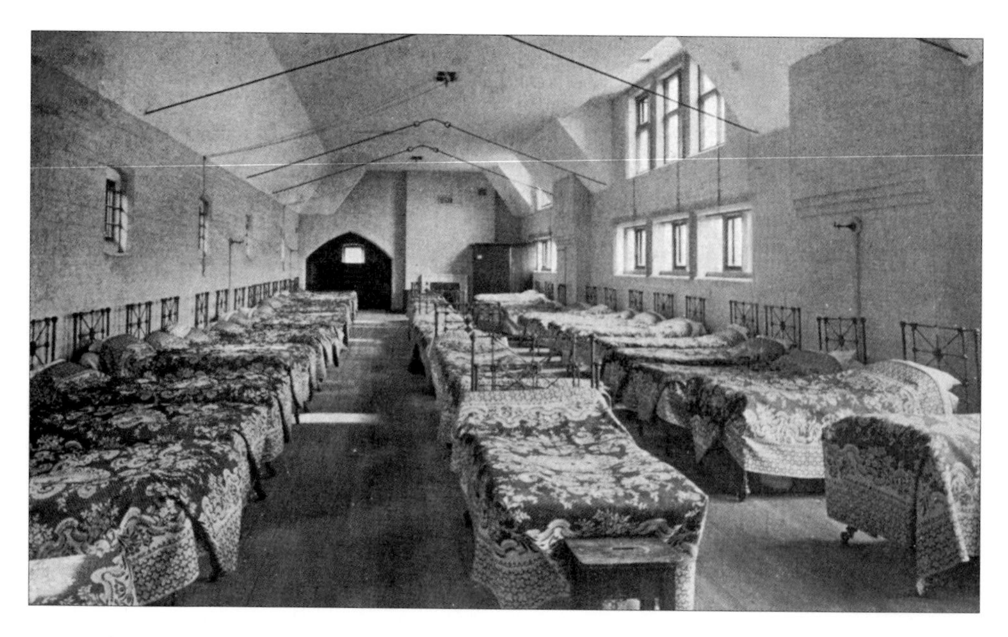

120 The 20th-century dormitory looks rather bare, despite the pretty coverlets—perhaps it was taken during a vacation.

121 The junior dormitories were built in 1916, facing south and with the railway at the left. In 1968 they were taken over by St Theresa's Roman Catholic School, and demolished in 1990 after that school had moved to new premises.

122 A sale brochure of 1901 has this picture of The Avenue at Hatch End, looking towards Uxbridge Road. No. 19 at the right, named 'Fairholme', shows the size of the plots. Though this and every house seen along the right had intensive redevelopment, several of the saplings survive as huge trees.

123 The owner of 25 The Avenue is probably thinking about King Canute as he contemplates the flood on Sunday 8 May 1988.

124 There was no Roman Catholic church in the Hatch End area before St Teresa of the Child Jesus opened near Headstone Lane in 1953, so the chapel in the Convent of Our Lady of Lourdes was used for Sunday worship. The Convent came to Hatch End in 1910, took over two large houses in Oxhey Lane—Oxhey Grove in 1915, and the adjoining Clonard in 1925—and ran a small school, replaced by an old people's home, until 1968. Many of the sequoia trees from Clonard stand about the replacement roads, giving the name Sequoia Park to one of them.

125 This is really a portrait of a beloved car—a Rover 12 Tourer with soft top, in two tones of blue, made in 1936. T.L.J. Bentley bought it in summer 1939 and treasured it until 1979. It is still on the road, a tribute to its cossetted life. Here it is, in summer 1939, parked in Headstone Lane. The distant houses are 1-5 Letchford Terrace, and the nearer ones hide *The Letchford Arms*. In 1950 Hatch End High School was built at the right.

126 The low cottage at the centre was built *c.*1650, and stood alone on the triangle at The Chantry until the little estate was built around it in sympathetic style soon after 1900. It met its end in the 1950s, while Hatch End High School was being built in Headstone Lane behind the camera.

127 The railway put up this row of cottages for its workers at the beginning of the 20th century, opposite the old house in The Chantry. After they were demolished *c.*1972, the site from here to Headstone Lane Station was used for light industry, as the notice advertises.

Above: **128** An anonymous sketch of St John's Church, dated 12 September 1837, shows the churchyard in the unkempt state alleged to be general at that time. There is no lofty Loudun monument, proving that it must have been erected nearer to the death of his widow Agnes in 1841 than to that of William in 1809, as is usually claimed. The pipe emerging from the chancel window ventilates the stove that warms the church. It will be 22 years before the Lady Chapel is built beside the chancel.

Left: **129** Most noticeable in this interior view of the church about the same time are the box pews, extending even into the chancel, and the internal part of the flue that ventilates the stove through the window. The wall there has not yet been removed for the Lady Chapel. The requisite Royal Arms are still fixed over the chancel arch and the ceiling timbers are covered.

Right: **130** Walter Llwarch Williams would have known those two views well. He is the longest-serving minister of Pinner so far—1764 to 1810, and from 1766 was also Vicar of Harrow. He could afford to live in Pinner House, rather than in the smaller vicarage next door.

Below left: **131** John Procter was a member of Pinner Vestry in 1788, qualified probably by his tenancy of Church Farm. Later he was a member of the Workhouse Committee, organiser of the Sunday School (which taught reading and writing) from 1799-1805, and churchwarden from 1811-14. His headstone stands in the churchyard.

Above right: **132** John Venn, incumbent of Pinner from 1830-3, urged local employers to pay their employees' wages by Saturday morning at the latest, so that shops need not open on Sundays. He gave the coloured glass windows in the porch of St John's.

133 This was the vicarage rejected by Williams, though there may have been subsequent modifications. In 1920 the Rev. Claude Rowlands used some of its 18 rooms as a school, which matured into St John's School. A new vicarage was built behind it in 1937-8.

134 Opposite the church, to the right of Church Cottage, stood this house, built *c.*1600 but long subdivided into two. Here, around 1920, James Rackliffe stands at the door of one with his granddaughter Olive. By now about seventy years old, he had helped manage *The Oddfellows Arms*, been a partner in the cab firm of Wilson & Rackliffe and run a sweet shop in Bridge Street.

135 Pinner House in Church Lane was once the home of the Rev. Walter Williams. In 1947 the side of the house towards Blackgates had a coat of creeper, the side door had a verandah and there was a tennis court. To the right is a corner of the huge garden, upon which sheltered housing and Ingle Close have been built. Pinner church tower is visible beyond the front of the house, unobscured by trees.

136 Here is one of the principal bedrooms in Pinner House, not during private occupation, but between 1948 and 1966, when it was a home for the elderly.

137 At the corner of Church Lane and Nower Hill stood the stables of Elmdene, with coachman's accommodation overhead. Outside them in 1898 waits coachman Charles Sherwell at the reins of a fine equipage, ready to go round to the house and pick up the owner, Frederick Dunbar Thomas. The building was converted into one residence about 1950 and called Elmdene Cottage.

138 Across the green stood The Cottage, the remnant of an old house or barn, adapted as a cottage and occupied until 1939. The site was about nos 201-3 Moss Lane.

139 The tradesman's cart across the green may have been delivering to one of these houses. Nower Hill House at the right looks across Moss Lane to The Fives Court sometime between the two world wars. The green is now called Tooke's Green because of the fountain at the left, erected to the memory of William Tooke in the 1880s.

Above and below: **140** At the back of The Fives Court (built 1899) was an integral court for playing the game of fives, hence the name of the house—it was between the two sloping roofs shown in the picture below. The house was built for Ambrose Heal junior to the designs of his cousin Cecil Brewer, the Arts and Crafts architect, and enlarged about 1909, after the date of this picture. The boy in the paddock is Cecil Heal, killed on active service in 1915, aged eighteen.

141 Edith Heal takes some exercise on the fives court in about 1910. Her husband, Ambrose Heal junior, was managing director of the furniture store Heal's in Tottenham Court Road.

142 East End had its complement of Victorian cottages. In 1911 the weekly rents of the four in this row were half as much again as those at West End, because these were built of brick. They were demolished *c.*1943, and in 1970 nos 33-36 Chiswick Court were built over the site.

Left: **143** Henry Hedges and his wife sit by the Tudor front porch of East End Farm with grandson Tony in summer 1932. Henry, his father William, grandfather James before him, and his son Sidney after him, lived in the ancient cottage and ran the farm until, by the late 1930s, house-building had eaten up the fields around and Sidney moved on to Woodhall Farm. Henry died in 1936.

Below: **144** The man in the top hat seems to be a uniformed coachman on duty among those attending the opening of the new Baptist Church in Paines Lane in 1910, the old one in Marsh Road having proved too small. In the same year its name was changed to Pinner United Free Church, aiming to discourage the formation of denominational bodies too small to be viable. Samuel Lammas Dore of Pinner Hill House had helped lay the foundation stone.

145 Who now remembers the tiny chapel in the middle of the Paines Lane cemetery, or the Nonconformist Chapel at the back, both pulled down in 1982? Once the cemetery was full they fell out of use, suffering consequent decay and vandalism.

146 Weatherley's Farm, about the site of 49-51 Paines Lane, was a farmhouse built *c.*1600. In 1748 a 16-year-old from here, John White, was killed in an altercation with gamekeeper James Wood, who was sentenced to be branded on the hand. James Hedges began his farming career here a century later.

Above: **147** William Barber, the landlord, replaced Weatherley's with Oakfield in 1887, for use as a small private school by Miss Florence Thompson and her sister Jane. About thirty youngsters from some of the 'best' local families attended, giving it cachet. It closed upon the death of Florence, and was shortly afterwards demolished for replacement.

148 William Barber was a judge, the teetotaller who had built the *Cocoa Tree Tavern* at the top of the High Street in 1878. He was president of Pinner Cricket Club, and to encourage local youth to participate he sometimes allowed cricket matches in his grounds at Barrow Point House, Paines Lane. Barber is said to be the man on the front of this concert programme.

149 In 1924 St John's School moved to Barrow Point House, once the home of William Barber. The front wing was severely damaged by fire in October 1930, fortunately at night after the boys had gone home, though it was the headmaster's 10-year-old son who gave the alarm. People are taking a look at the damage. The school stayed here until 1970.

150 Waxwell Farm stands solitary in Waxwell Lane, already a gentleman's residence rather than a farmhouse. The date of the photo is not known, but must be before 1894, when Edward Trotter began the large extension at the left and started to expose the timber framework. The lane is narrow and little beyond it is visible, though the Wax Well must be within the further bushes. At the right, fields gradually slope down to the Pinn.

151 Trotter's additions at the rear of Waxwell Farm are visible at the right. Many more have been made since the premises were taken over in 1947 by The Grail, a Catholic movement concerned with ecumenical and welfare work. At the left is accommodation for residential courses, while the round apse of the chapel dominates the centre.

152 A postman collects the mail from the postbox at the corner of Love Lane, right, and Waxwell Lane. This is 1926 and 60-6 Waxwell Lane are about twenty years old. The distant white house beyond the postman may be in Oakhill Avenue, for the higher part of Barrow Point Avenue in between has not yet been laid out.

153 Volunteer fireman Beaumont proudly shows off the Pinner fire engine, a manual one, polished and painted, at the old coach house in Waxwell Lane, which was the first fire station. It used to adjoin Orchard Cottage. This is either Walter Henry Beaumont, who lived next door at Glastonbury Villa, between the coach house and Bee Cottage, or his older brother George William of the High Street, who were alternate foremen of the fire brigade. The date is probably a few years before a new engine and fire station were provided in 1903.

154 The first Roman Catholic Church of St Luke in Love Lane is here seen all alone. Built in 1915, plans to extend it were overtaken by the building of a new church alongside it in 1957 in a contrasting style, leaving this one to be used as parish rooms.

155 Almost opposite St Luke's stood Wilby House, 39 Love Lane, with its unusual attic window, built about 1896 by Joseph Petley, the grocer at 9 High Street. For a few years from 1937 the Sisters of Charity ran a small school in it. It suffered a serious fire in 1964, and was demolished to provide the entrance to the car park.

156 The view from the Metropolitan Railway's Harrow Garden Village estate to Rayners Lane Station predates the station rebuilding of 1937. The shops are at the northern corner of Rayners Lane and Village Way, while sand and stacks of bricks are ready for building houses in The Close. The great elms mark the old line of Rayners Lane, and the grass verge was retained for them but, alas, they were killed by Dutch elm disease in the 1980s.

157 It looks as though minor repairs are being made to the 'up' platform of the old Rayners Lane Station this day in 1933, or soon after. Most of the platform name signs have the solid diamond backgrounds of the Metropolitan Railway, but there at the right is the bar and circle preferred by other lines, which the London Transport Passenger Board adopted after it took over the underground lines in 1933. The poster at the left advertises Gracie Fields in a show at The Coliseum.

158 The Tithe Farm Estate built south of the Piccadilly Line by T. Nash Ltd was a huge undertaking. This picture of one of the terraces going up also shows that even on the cheaper estates individual features, such as the hipped roof of one house, could be chosen by purchasers.

159 Nash had a toy-like railway track all over his estate for the early stages of development, but horses were still necessary for the more detailed later stages. The line of carts is in Alexandra Avenue at the end of Clitheroe Avenue and flats will be built on either side of the main road. The blocks in the right foreground are the upside-down capitals of the divisions between shop fronts.

160 The cinema at Rayners Lane is listed Grade II*, a bold and simple Art Deco work of 1936 by F.E. Bromige. The whole of this scene, photographed in 1974, six years before the cinema closed, has become part of Rayners Lane Conservation Area. In 2000 the cinema was acquired, restored and refurbished as a Zoroastrian Community Centre and Place of Worship, and named as the Zoroastrian Centre for Europe.

161 The fittings of the cinema foyer are also listed. The flat metal balustrades round the sunken centre of the foyer and up the stairs (not shown) share the Art Deco style. So does the lower half of the period mirror at the rear left. In the cinema's early days there were tables and chairs in the well for afternoon tea.

162 and **163** Right at the southern end of Cannon Lane, beside Roxbourne Park, was a pocket of less salubrious activity. A sewage works was established there in 1880 and stayed until superseded by the west Middlesex sewage works at Mogden in 1936, whereupon Harrow Council used its space as a plant nursery. In 1924 the Pinner Gas Company replaced its gas holder in Eastcote Road with a larger one north of the sewage farm and a smaller one was added after the war by the Gas, Light and Coke Co., which had taken over in 1929. In the late 1980s Harrow Council closed the nursery and North Thames Gas vacated the holder station soon afterwards. The site was decontaminated and, on the joint site, in the late 1990s, Royale Crescent and its associated roads rose up.

The pictures were taken in 1974, the one of the nursery from the top of the gasholder. Yeading Avenue is on the horizon to the left, and Castleton Road (in Eastcote) is to the right.

164 As Cannon Lane north of Village Way grew around it, Downs Farmhouse was stranded. The Methodist Church bought it in 1956, and over the next 20 years gradually replaced the premises with its own buildings. In this picture of September 1972, the last old remnants—the farmhouse and shed—are crowded by the church hall behind, and were pulled down not long afterwards.

165 North Harrow Station was opened as a little wooden station in 1915. The proper station entrance, in the 20th-century livery of biscuit-coloured tiles, came a little later. There have been a few changes to this scene of 1933: now you must enter round the other side of the bridge, while the houses advertised on it cost a little more than £850 these days. If only buses were as plentiful now ...

166 Cinemas were the flagship buildings of the inter-war suburbs. In cream tiles like the Langham in Pinner, but rather more grand in style, the Embassy at North Harrow opened in 1929 and lasted 34 years, closing in 1963 to make way for a supermarket and bowling alley. The flowerbeds have long gone.

167 The bowling alley was popular, but closed in 2005 together with the supermarket, which had been abandoned by the Morrison chain when it took over Safeway, to be cleared away in favour of a dense housing scheme.

Left: **168** The deep snow of January 1939 covers the fast disappearing fields. No. 25 Highfield Avenue, whose garden wall is in the foreground, seems to be the outpost of civilisation, but there are houses in the far gloom, in Cannon Lane. The tall trees border the Yeading Brook. The man is walking along Whittington Way, which has been laid out but not yet built up—the sign advertises that the houses will cost a quite expensive £925.

Below: **169** The ancient Headstone Manor was a working dairy farm until 1925 and the farmyard is here being used for its traditional purpose. The two cows in the foreground are making for the access slope to the moat at the right, to drink or cool their feet. There is no such access now. The 14th-century wing of the house is hidden by trees at the right, and creeper is trained up the Georgian façade of the 16th-century part.

170 A woman stands beside the moat at Headstone Manor a century ago, and is reflected in its waters together with the poplars and haystacks. She carries a muff, for it is winter. One stack has already been half used, but there seem to be another four left. The moat has railings these days, and the rick yard is the car park.

171 The 150ft-long great barn of Headstone Manor is pictured in its Second World War guise of theatre, part of the holidays at home campaign, perhaps. Could that be a ticket kiosk at the right? The texture of the lovely old roof shows up beautifully in what is another of T.L.J. Bentley's photographs.

Left: **172** Before it was adapted as a theatre, the barn was used as a store for all sorts of things. The interior was photographed in 1942 and highlights the stout framework, which dates from 1506.

Below: **173** Hay ricks were still to be seen in Pinner 50 years ago. These were just off George V Avenue on the fields of Hall's Farm, more anciently known as Pinner Park Farm. It began as a 13th-century deer reserve called Pinner Park, and was converted into a farm in the 16th century. The old farmhouse was rebuilt *c.*1750, the farm buildings some 50-80 years later. Its tall granary has been reinstalled at Headstone Manor. The farmer moved away in the 1990s, and now the farm buildings are used for other purposes, while the fields are rented out for grazing. The 230-acre farm was scheduled as open space in 1930, and belongs to the local council.

Above: **174** The hay was for Farmer Hall's dairy herd, some of which await milking beside the early 19th-century Dutch barn in 1977.

Right: **175** A tanker siphons the milk from the rotary milking parlour in 1966. People were welcome to climb the stairs to the upper gallery and watch the milking, and quite a few local youngsters discovered the link between cows and milk up there. The parlour still stands, but unused.

176 Hall's Farm used to bottle and deliver its own milk, the bottling plant being in part of this big shed where the milk floats are taking their ease.

177 These two tied cottages are still at Hall's Farm, though they are hard to recognise now. They were a pair of Victorian back-to-backs, two up, two down, with the door in the gable wall and outside toilets. Now they are derelict, the windows out, the little gardens gone. Just in front of the further trees George V Avenue will one day be laid across the farm fields.

Right: **178** Thomas Ellement (1877-1957) volunteered for the Boer War and went out to South Africa with the Imperial Yeomanry as a trooper. Here he is—hatless—somewhere in the veldt. Lord Kitchener's dispatches mention that in April 1901 Corporal Ellement 'with five men drove off a party of Boers and attacked a convoy with great determination, thereby saving six wagons'.

Below: **179** *The Queen's Head* is helping an army recruiting drive in September 1914, very soon after the outbreak of the First World War. All the advertisements call for enlisters—on the pub wall at the left Britannia stretches out her arms saying 'Men! Your country needs you.' The picture at the kerb, repeated on the wall behind, highlights the 'Mounted Branches'. The sign painted on the horse trough points to a recruiting office, probably in the old parish hall at the foot of the street.

Left: **180** Whether Ernie Rackliffe (1880-1947) responded to that particular call is not known, but here he is, a lance bombardier in the Royal Artillery, enjoying a smoke during time out in France. The snap forms a postcard, on which he wrote in pencil 'To my big boy from your loving Dad. Somewhere in France. 28th April 1918.' It is addressed to his son Ben, aged eight, and probably went by military bag. Ernie, the eldest son of James, was variously a railwayman, a chauffeur and a publican at *The Oddfellows Arms*.

Above: **181** Alan Dore, a son of Samuel Lammas Dore, grew up at Pinner Hill House. He joined the 7th Battalion, Worcester Regiment, B.E.F. and became a flier, ending the First World War as a major with a D.S.O. and bar. In later life he became Deputy Lord Lieutenant of Middlesex.

Left: **182** Edwin Ware, successor to Jimmy Bedford as parish clerk, was in the 133rd Field Ambulance Unit, R.A.M.C. and was often a stretcher bearer. He was wounded twice. He is standing in this photo taken at a studio in Waton, Belgium in 1917.

183 There was a convalescent hospital in Pinner Place for war-wounded servicemen, and local people often welcomed them into their homes for tea, or helped provide teas, parties or small entertainments for them. Here is a group of wounded, their helpers (some in Guide or similar uniform) and children in the playground in School Lane around the end of the First World War, or soon after it.

184 Civil Defence was a very important part of the war effort during the Second World War. These are the air raid wardens of Post 35 in the park off Whittington Way.

185 George Bendall, Head Fire Guard of Pinner, makes the best of it at Warden Post 32 in West Way.

186 A land mine flattened the corners of East Towers and Eastcote Road on 16 October 1940, killing three people. By the time this photo was taken from a point in East Towers, the rubble had been cleared and the damaged roof of 2 Rochester Drive at the far right repaired. The houses were rebuilt very soon after the war and are hardly distinguishable from the others.

187 A V1 flying bomb shattered a large number of houses in Parkside Way near Pinner View on 21 June 1944, killing six people. This was no. 106. Some furniture has survived, and a man salvages an armful of books. There is a makeshift brazier on the grass verge.

188 Another flying bomb devastated part of Cumberland Road at North Harrow on 30 June 1944, causing five deaths. Here is the wreckage of what were probably nos 53-5, with 49-51 gutted at the left.

189 There was constant fundraising for needy causes during the war. After one campaign, which raised £500 plus, two stretcher ambulances were bought and given to the Red Cross in April 1941. A ceremony was held at the War Memorial, when the ignition keys were handed to Lady Symonds, President of the Middlesex Red Cross, by Edward Montesole, President of the Pinner Ambulance Fund, who lived at East House.

Below left: **190** This is one of Bert Thomas's cartoons in aid of fundraising for Red Cross parcels for British prisoners-of-war in German camps, featuring his favourite indomitable Tommy.

Above: **191** Bert Thomas was a cartoonist of national status who had lived at Church Farm for many years. He moved away in 1944, not long after one of his sons was killed on active service.

Above: **192** Rota was a cuddly lion cub won in a bet by George Thompson of Cuckoo Hill Road, who kept him in a cage in the garden. When war came he was fully grown, and had no ration book! Thompson boarded him at the London Zoo and then in 1943 gave him to Winston Churchill. Here Churchill, with Thompson at the right, and Mrs Thompson, is feeding Rota.

Right: **193** At the zoo Rota was the mighty progenitor of 30 cubs. This picture shows him presiding over the notice of three new ones in 1945, whose names—Monty, Ike and Waaf—perhaps reflect Churchill's interest.

194 Pinner Fair flourished during the war, though it had to close before dark. The three wooden cottages beside the river in Chapel Lane form the backdrop of several stalls in 1940. The Round Table has pinned up a picture of Nazis dropping down on Pinner by parachute as targets for a game of darts.

195 Have these two girls spent all their pocket money at Pinner Fair, or are they still deciding? The gables showing above the roundabouts belong to the shops in Bridge Street that curve round to Love Lane. The date must be *c.*1916.

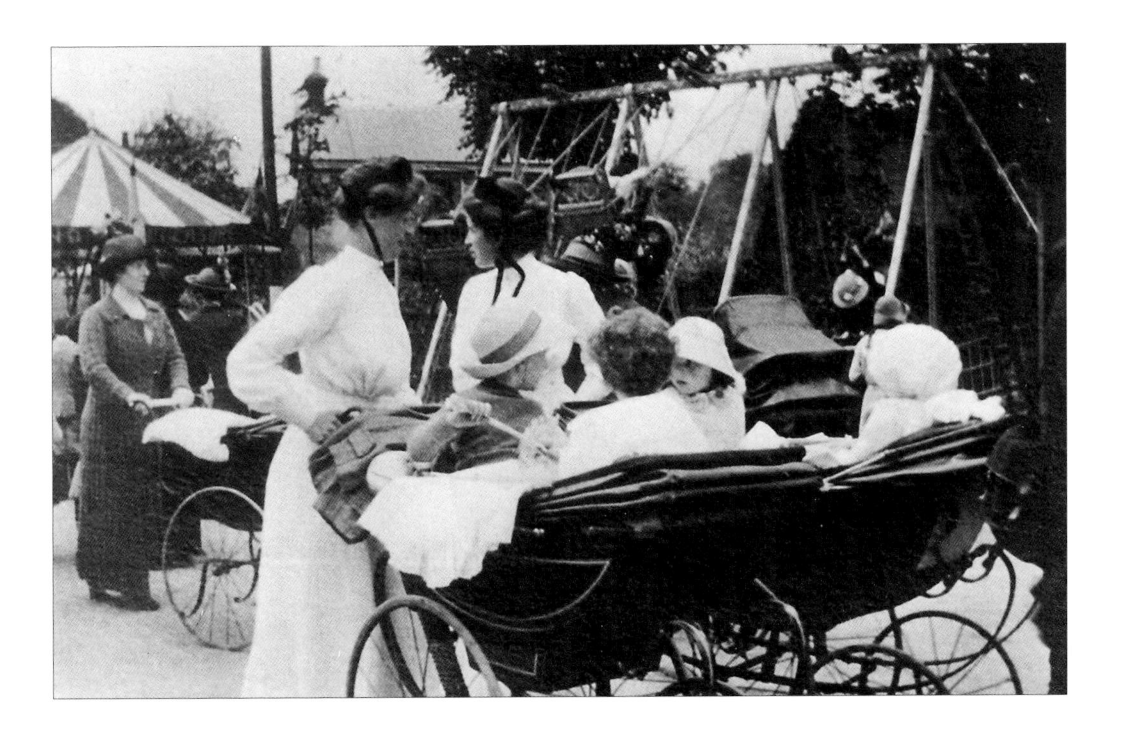

Above: **196** Perhaps kiddies' attractions are the reason for this cluster of four prams at the top of the High Street during the fair of about 1912. The two pushers in the foreground look like nursemaids taking the opportunity to gossip, and their charges are doing the same.

Right: **197** No one is too young to lend a hand at the fair! A little gypsy looks after the popcorn close to the caravans sometime during the 1920s.

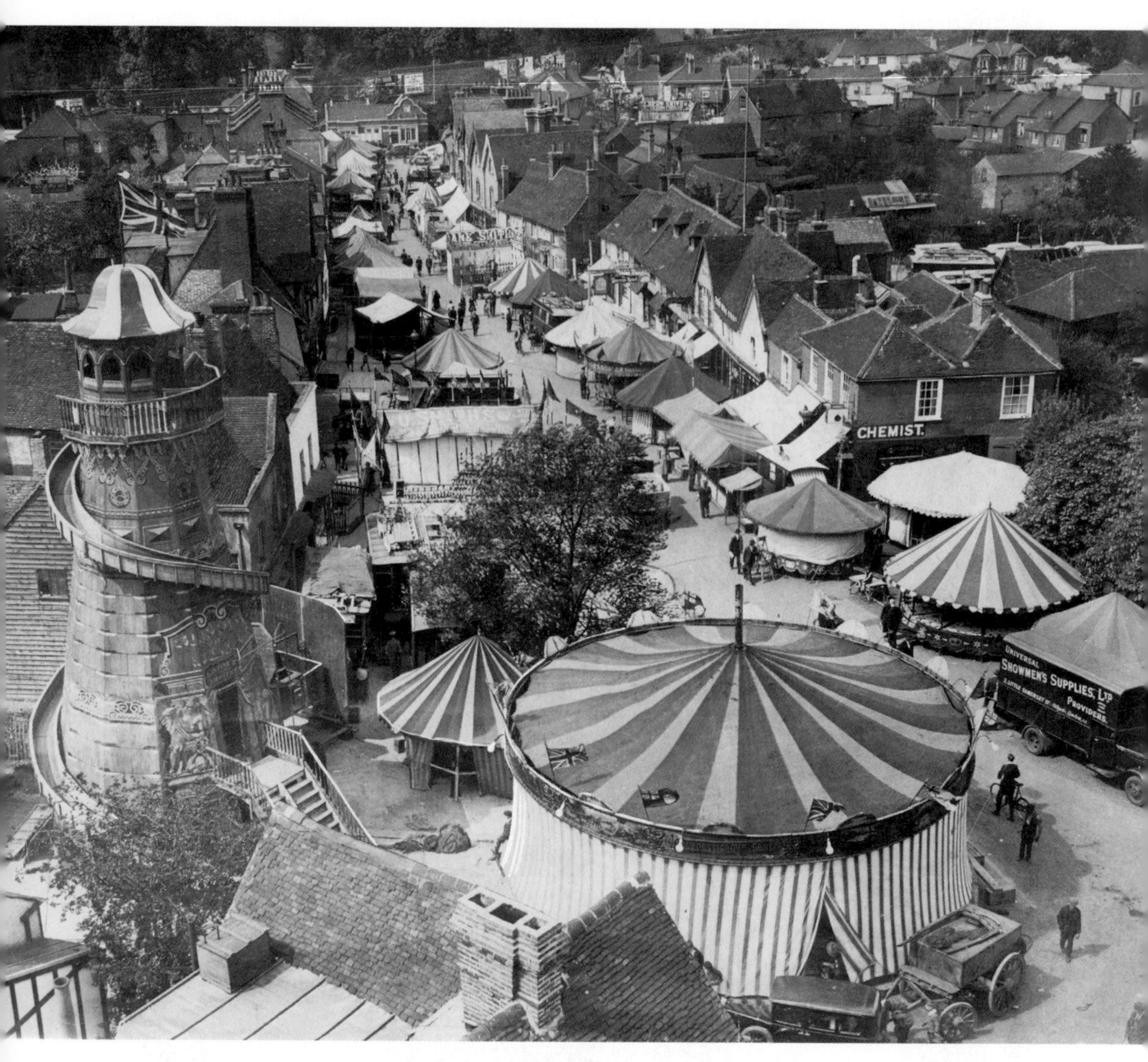

198 Pinner Fair is pictured just before opening time in 1932. The highly decorated helter-skelter has its Union Jack flying upside-down, and the roundabout in the foreground looks smart enough to be Henry V's pavilion at Agincourt. At the foot of the High Street is the former school, with cottages in Chapel Lane to the right and then the newsagent's shop at the corner of the lane, behind Albert Smith's coconut shy. The space behind *The Queen's Head* is full of showmen's vehicles, and it is surprising to see how many outbuildings and cottages were stuffed into the area between the High Street and Bridge Street.

199 This could be the earliest picture of Pinner footballers, taken on the Pinner Green Cricket Ground, which became Montesole Playing Fields. Pinner Football Club was founded in 1892. The First Eleven for 1897-8 are, from left to right: P. Carter, T. Barnes, J. Butterfield, C. Parkhouse, W. Carter, W. Bugden, C. Bugden, W. Woodman, T. Deer, T. Ellement, A. Petley. The photographer was the captain, C. Stone.

200 Here are the Top Hats v. Bonnets football teams of 1898, some of whom can be identified from the previous picture. This must be at a festivity or fundraising activity.

201 This is the Pinner F.C. Eleven of 1907, fielding three footballing Gregory brothers, all of whom played for Watford F.C. Owen, second left at the back, never advanced beyond amateur at Watford. Frederick or 'Faye', middle row, extreme right, was a professional at Watford by 1911, and captain for three seasons, usually playing full-back or half-back. Afterwards, from 1926-37, he was licensee of the old *Victory*. Next to him sits Val, professional at Watford in 1911, who captained Wolverhampton Wanderers in the FA Cup final of 1921, losing to Tottenham Hotspur.

202 The Pinner Ladies' Hockey Club First Eleven of 1909-10 also contained relatives—Mrs Light, extreme right in the middle row, and her 19-year-old daughter Hilda sitting beside her. They lived in Devonshire Road at Hatch End, and Hilda's first school was Oakfield in Paines Lane. She played county and national hockey, captaining both her county and England in 1924.

203 A Pinner tennis club breaks for tea in the Edwardian period.

204 This looks like a competition or match day at the tennis club about 1930.

205 There is a little skittering as Pinner Drag Hunt moves down the High Street in 1933, probably on Boxing Day. In the lead is the Master, Fred Hall of Hall's Farm.

206 The whipper-in marshals the hounds of the Pinner Drag Hunt outside the now vanished *Headstone Hotel* opposite the station at North Harrow, presumably waiting for the hunters to come over from Hall's Farm. The hotel advertises a ballroom for hire, dining hall, lounge, tea gardens and putting green.

Above: **207** Film stars! The Pinner Drag Hunt 'meets' on the film set of an Irish village at Twickenham Studios, for the filming of The Lily of Killarney, in September 1933. The rider at the extreme left looks like Violet Hall, daughter of Fred Hall, the Hunt Master. She later married Cyril Ellement. It is probably Fred next to her.

Right: **208** Edward VIII joined the Middlesex Farmers' Hunt on one occasion (probably while still Prince of Wales) and is here seen chatting on what is said to be the area of Downs Farm.

209 Pinner Horse Show and Gymkhana was held for many years after the Second World War, usually at the old football field at the end of Cuckoo Hill Road. Notables like Alan Oliver competed. The winners of the driving turn-out competition in 1957 were Pell and Mell, held here by their driver, who drew the coach of Queen Salote of Tonga to the coronation of Queen Elizabeth II in 1953. The small horse is their stable companion, King Size.

210 This is probably election day 1910 and the competing posters are on view. Some cry 'The radicals are taxing our food', 'Lest we forget', 'Support old Gladstonian principles of finance by voting for your Unionist candidate', 'Mallaby Deeley' (he was the Conservative candidate). The people outside *The Queen's Head* look a good deal more businesslike than the usual Pinner onlookers.

211 Daniel Gurney, owner of *The Victory*, died in 1906 leaving a very large sum to 'the poor of Pinner'. It was eventually distributed at *The Queen's Head* in 1925 (surely it should have been at *The Victory*) when, according to the *Daily Mirror*, 300 people received a share. These may be some of the beneficiaries.

212 The horse bus service, operated by the mainline railway between Pinner village and Hatch End Station, ran from 25 May 1885 till 30 April 1916. It carried eight inside and two outside by the driver, George Bridge, at a fare of four old pence. Here is George, resting his horses—there are three hind legs—outside the old *Bell* at Pinner Green.

213 Manpower is needed to get a 183 bus moving in the snows of 1962. *The Red Lion* did not last the year out. Its forecourt, so useful for buses to turn round in, was built over, and now the buses turn around at the end of Love Lane.

214 What looks like a Type 5 BR locomotive, no. 60815, puffs through Pinner Station about 1947 on its way to Marylebone. Not until 1961 were the two additional tracks completed, allowing Marylebone trains to bypass the station. The old down platform pictured at the left was rebuilt as a consequence.

215 To celebrate the centenary of Pinner Station in May 1985, Pinner Local History Society took over part of it for three days. More than 400 people booked seats on a specially organised commemorative train (modern) to travel round parts of the old Metropolitan track. Most were dressed in period costume, delighting and puzzling ordinary travellers at designated alighting points. The man raising his boater is the organiser-in-chief, Ted Hayden, then chairman of the society.

216 Pinner is home to many people in the entertainment industry, some of whom lend their pulling power to local events. In May 1981 Bob Holness and Ronnie Barker shared the heavy task of laying the foundation stone of the new hall of the Pinner & District Community Association, although the stone gives all the credit to Barker.

217 A pancake-race in aid of charity was occasionally held in the High Street in the later 20th century, the last being organised by local restaurateurs in 1996. This is the 1984 race with Ronnie Barker—in his trademark striped blazer—signalling 'Thataway!'

218 It is December 1961, and snow has deadened and emptied the dual carriageway of St Thomas's Drive. Just here, looking towards North Harrow, the modern houses end and beyond them the old medieval Pinner Park slopes away in the gloom.

Index

Entries referring to the Introduction have a Roman page number, while entries referring to illustration captions have the caption's Arabic numeral.